MAKING THE CITY A
BETTER PLACE

DAVID K. KOOP, D.MIN.

Dedication

I dedicate this book to my wife, Cheryl,
who has been my partner in life and ministry, since 1978

Table of Contents

Acknowledgments

First and foremost, I would like to thank my Lord and Savior Jesus Christ for granting me the strength and grace for this project. He has always demonstrated that He believes in me, and His Holy Spirit has encouraged me through many challenging moments.

Next, I would like to thank my wife Cheryl and our four children, Jennifer, Matthew, Chelsea, and Lacey, for their love, patience, and understanding throughout my ministry and during this project. I also owe much to my parents who cheered me on and extended their support.

It would also be appropriate to thank the many wonderful people at Coastal Church, Vancouver, British Columbia. They have loved and supported my family with the love of Christ for the past twenty years. Thanks to our church staff, whose input was crucial, and to the Board of Directors, who have given me liberty in time and finances to pursue this endeavor.

Over the years I have been blessed to have many wonderful mentors, teachers and friends, who have each in their own way inspired me. The greatest influence was my father, Henry Koop, who is with the Lord today after faithfully living a life that exemplified Christ. I would like to give a special thank you to Dr. Peter Van Breda and Dr. Ray Bakke, who gave me the encouragement I needed to take on this project; and a special thanks to Jennifer Ennis, and Karen Wong who helped tirelessly on book edits. You and numerous unnamed others have enriched me more than words can say.

Preface

In 2004 my good friend Pastor Peter Van Breda asked me to consider doing a Doctorate of Ministry at Bakke Graduate School of Ministry. Considering my work schedule and family life, I felt that it was out of reach. However, he encouraged me that it would be well worth the effort, and that it was an opportunity to study what God was doing at Coastal Church in an academic setting knowing I would learn from other leaders around the world.

One of the greatest benefits of doing these studies was to take the Coastal Church family along on the journey. Much of what I discovered and learned has been woven into the fabric of the church giving us a richer and broader perspective. I have compiled this special 20th anniversary book from the dissertation I submitted for my doctorate. The goal of telling the story is to bring both inspiration and information about the planting and growth of a vibrant church in the heart of the city. My prayer is that the story of Coastal Church will help us all see that the Holy Spirit is at work in our cities, and gives us confidence to trust our Lord in boldly sharing the Gospel.

In this book I have included several testimonies of lives that have been transformed by the grace of God at Coastal Church. They are just a sampling of the thousands of lives that have been changed. The transformation of an urban center will happen one heart at a time. My prayer is that these stories and the lessons I have learned will inspire you to reach the cities of the world today.

Foreword

It is an honor to be asked to write the foreword to this testimonial about the work of God among a people in the City of Vancouver. As the supervising professor I had the distinct privilege of overseeing Dave's doctoral dissertation, which is the inspiration for this book. This is the story of how God goes about His work in the 'City.'

My wife, Gabriella, and I had known the Koop family since 1993. They had come from the prairies of Canada and our family had come from South Africa. I believe it was a "God engineered" encounter – both families being new transplants to the city of Vancouver.

The Hebrew word translated "city" refers to any human settlement surrounded by a fortification or wall. There are 1,250 uses of the word city in scripture. Suburbs on the other hand are defined a smaller community adjacent to or within commuting distance of a city and are by enlarge single-use areas – where places to live, work, play, and learn are separated from one another. What makes a city is the close proximity of residences, workplaces, and cultural institutions which of necessity bring about more person-to-person interactions. Dave's book is about those connections, and how relationships in relation to a loving Savior, can and does happen in the city of Vancouver.

The growth of large cities represent not only challenges, but also opportunities for the church of Jesus Christ. The book outlines both the challenges and the tremendous opportunities in relation to working with God in the City.

Statistics show that now over half the world live in cities. In the modern connected world we live in, the cities presence impacts everyone. Not only those who live and work in the city, but also places far from large cities are influenced. It is out of the cities that financial, cultural, personal and spiritual impact flows.

The challenges the church in the city faces are firstly demographic as more and more people from very diverse cultural and economic backgrounds migrate to the cities of the world and Vancouver, being a gateway city, is no exception.

Because the majority of the world's non-Christians do not only reside in foreign lands, but these culturally distant peoples now are our neighbours in the city, the second challenge is missiological. Dr. Ray Bakke has said *"you don't have to cross the ocean to do missions, you need only cross the street as God has drawn the nations of the world to the cities"*

Thirdly, the challenge for the church in our cities is Apostolic as we seek to minister the gospel of Jesus Christ to a hurt and dying people living in the cities.

Finally, the challenge is financial. It goes without saying that the costs associated with a church in the city are astronomical and present an ever present challenge as the church seeks to minister effectively in the city.

The untold story of Coastal Church is that even although each of the above four challenges are ever present, the pastors of Coastal Church are effectively managing the resources entrusted to them. They are ably led by Dave and Cheryl and as they diligently steward the multiplied giftings of the congregation, the people resources, and financial contributions entrusted to them by the Lord.

Psalm 107:7 "He led them also by a straight way, that they might go to a city of habitation. (KJ21)

And so it was into the city of Vancouver that Dr. David Koop, Cheryl, and their four young children were thrust by God.

This is the story of that journey as they came to establish a credible, living testimony for the Lord Jesus Christ. *Matthew 5:14 "Ye are the light of the world. A city that is set on a hill cannot be hid."*

The book tells of how this great church is a refuge for the sick, the oppressed, the brokenhearted, the lost, and all those who seek a genuine encounter with the living God. From the beginning it has been a journey of faith where countless people told them it could not be done. It has been reported that over twenty previous attempts at church plants in downtown Vancouver have not succeeded.

So the question to ask is what made this different?

I believe there are numerous things that contributed to this and I have attempted to capture a few of them to briefly describe this amazing family:

1. The grace and mercy of a loving God
2. The Apostolic calling God for the city placed on this family
3. Their unwavering faith in the midst of trials and setbacks
4. The lessons of childhood – growing up on a farm in Alberta where the principles of sowing and reaping were well learnt
5. The tenacity, consistency, and unwavering commitment to the city of Vancouver and their calling to the people of this great city

So it is with great joy that I congratulate Coastal Church and Dave, Cheryl, and the family on this twenty year milestone. We continue to pray for you as you push back the boundaries of the enemy and be the light in a dark place.

Vancouver is as better place because of the unwavering commitment of this precious family to the city, to you (the people of Coastal Church), and to the nations of the world gathered right here in this city.

In His unfailing love
Dr Peter van Breda
Member of the Board of Directors
Coastal Church
Vancouver B.C.

Introduction

Over the phone came the caustic response, "What are you doing here? Can't you see all the stone churches downtown are cold and empty? Why don't you go out to the suburbs like the rest of them?" This response was given to a group of Bible school students attending the World Harvest School of Ministry, who had conducted a survey in the West End of Vancouver, Canada. The purpose of the study was to ascertain whether launching a new church in this community would succeed. Unlike the Downtown East Side (DTES) with its numerous soup kitchens and homeless shelters, the West End was a self-satisfied high-rise community that clearly sent a message for churches to stay out.

My wife, Cheryl, and I found ourselves leading this group of students into a mission field that we knew very little about. We both were raised in Christian homes on the prairies of Canada with rural backgrounds. Our spiritual journey had led us to leave our jobs in the corporate world and give our lives to church work. The survey of the land revealed a pocket of city dwellers with a vanishing Christian presence. In this setting, God was calling us to change the spiritual climate, and in doing so reveal transformational leadership principles. This book assesses the principles involved in the planting and survival of the urban church known as Coastal Church.

As the church grew, it became obvious that God was doing something unusual in the heart of Vancouver. While many of the traditional churches were struggling, Coastal Church was experiencing growth and a fresh excitement for God's word. The methodology that led to this growth for Coastal Church had never been studied and recorded. Dr. Bakke, an urban missiologist, challenged me that it was my responsibility to steward this journey for others and capture it for the next generation. In order to accomplish this task, I would need to understand the scope of what God is doing in cities around the world, with an academic dimension. To those who read this, it is my prayer that the lessons I have learned would resonate with you and inspire you to reach the cities of the world today.

The Congregation of Coastal Church

Coastal Church is situated in the international city of Vancouver, British Columbia. A 2011 National Household Survey by Statistics Canada revealed that 50.5 percent of the Vancouver population was foreign-born.[1] This diversity is represented in the church, which is comprised of over sixty different nationalities. Also represented in the congregation are a variety of social and economic backgrounds. The backgrounds include those who are struggling with poverty, to executives living and working in the downtown core. The church intentionally celebrates and cultivates diversity in music, food, the arts, and language. It is hoped that the reader will gain a greater understanding in how to work together in unity with various cultures.

The nature of our church in this type of urban setting tends to be much like an airport, with people landing and leaving for various reasons, such as business, education, and travel. These individuals make up about 30 percent of the Coastal Church congregation. In establishing a culture that is welcoming and accepting of people, no matter how long they stay, we encourage them to participate in church life. The experience they have at the church often leads to expanding the kingdom of Christ in their homelands. For example, there are those from Muslim countries that do not have the opportunity to hear the Gospel in their homeland, but have come to faith in Christ here. They return to their country, lead others to Christ, and establish small groups there. Others have come to the church and received discipleship training. This training has resulted in them planting churches in densely populated cities in other parts of the world.

Those living in the densely populated high-rise communities of world-class cities make up one of the greatest mission fields of this century. "For the first time in history, more than 50 percent of the world's people will live in urban areas. And the current rate of urbanization is such that, if it holds, the urban share of the global population could reach 60 percent by 2030, according to UN projections."[2] With city planners no longer designating space for churches, the high cost of meeting facilities and the overall negative perception of the church, it has become increasingly difficult for congregations to gain a foothold in the city. As my wife and I embarked on this great adventure, I soon discovered the lack of church planting material that would assist the pioneer endeavoring to establish a sustainable work in this challenging urban environment.

In this changing landscape the church must adapt. Faith-based organizations are in a state of flux today. Many of the older churches who once supported them are declining in attendance and influence within their communities. This situation has resulted in a drop in financial support and a shrinking volunteer base. Today, these organizations are being forced to adapt in how they reach the hurting and disadvantaged. As a result, the leaders of existing faith-based organizations are looking to identify with emerging churches. A number of these groups have approached Coastal Church to work with their leaders in an attempt to pool our knowledge and resources to help the hurting in our city.

Many of these groups have focused primarily on partnering with churches in the suburbs and have only recently come to see the trend of people moving back into the heart of the city. There has been a keen interest from the leaders of these groups to understand the different dynamics in the urban setting and what approach they should take in preparation to reach this segment of the population for Christ.

Jen's Story

When I moved to Vancouver "temporarily" around 2001, I decided I liked it here and had a mission to finally settle in and put some roots down after living in 10 places within 2 years in the Toronto area.

My goal was to find a place to live and stay awhile, get a good job and make some friends, create some stability, and then I'd be happy. I finally moved into an apartment in the West End where I would live a record number of consecutive years other than in my childhood home. My lifestyle was typical for someone living in the city in their 20s – my social life consisted of drinking with friends, clubbing, and on top of that I did not have healthy dating relationships, a pattern that had been established long before I moved here.

I do remember clearly that one day I was walking down Burrard St. downtown and noticed the churches. Part of me wanted to go in, and the other part said not to because I didn't want to be pressured if I did. I was told in university to steer clear of the Christians – they'd make you let go of your friends and the way you wanted to live your life. On the other hand, I felt like I didn't have a deep connection in the community, despite the fact I now had a home, a job, and friends as I'd set out to do. If I had left Vancouver at that moment, it would have made no difference to the city or the people.

Not long after, I met a man and was surprised to find out he was a Christian because he was so normal. I slowly gravitated toward him and we started dating. It was a tumultuous relationship. He kept referring to me as non-believer which drove me crazy. I did believe in God, I just didn't know very much about Him and didn't have a relationship with Him. We'd fight about it, because I didn't know if the things he was telling me were true. I became exasperated and told him to not talk to me about God anymore; I wanted it to be a non-topic in our relationship.

During this, I started attending the Alpha Course at Coastal Church because I couldn't refute anything that he said about God, the Bible, anything! I needed ammo. I think I was also curious or I wouldn't have gone. I went alone, and I remember the first night when I found a bench to sit on and engrossed myself in a book so I could avoid talking to anyone. In the periphery I could see 'the reverend' heading over to where I was, and thought "oh no". I tried to look very busy reading the book. Allan Burnett sat down beside, asked me a couple of non-intrusive questions to get to know me, and then moved on.

At Alpha I found a place where I could learn about Christianity, and no one put any pressure on me. Even when I told the group leader I didn't want to participate in the discussion, she said that was fine. I started warming up to the lady who'd write out our name tag every week. She was so welcoming and remembered my name before I even told her. As the course was ending she offered me an invitation to her small group that she hosted in her home. Years later she shared with me that it was a risk for her to invite me; she thought I might 'punch her out' if she asked. I don't think she literally thought I would do that, as much as describing the barbed wire aura I was putting up. Despite that, God was working in me powerfully during those weeks.

My boyfriend and I broke up during this time, and that was also my breaking point. The long weekend had just begun, and I faced days ahead of feeling upset and very alone. I didn't receive any phone calls or texts from friends, nothing. One night when

I was in bed, I reached up my hands, something I do NOT do, and told him that if having a relationship with Him meant not feeling alone anymore, that I wanted one. I heard a text message come in. The only one that whole weekend. It said "You're going to experience a powerful move of God this Sunday." It was my now ex-boyfriend – apparently he was still going to take me to church as we originally had planned.

On Sunday night we went, and during the service I could feel a response rise up in me. The altar call came, and we were at a church where you went up to the altar if you wanted to receive Christ as your Saviour. This was the complete opposite of my reserved personality to go up in front of everyone, but I knew I had to go.

After becoming a believer I started reading the beginner New Testament Bible I had been given, circling anything that confused me or I disagreed with. Thankfully over the years those pieces of Scripture started to make a lot more sense to me through sermons and various Bible School courses that I took.

I was excited to start volunteering at Coastal and asked my first church friend if she thought they'd take me. She was pretty sure they would. I joined the Children's Ministry team, and soon was asked to be the leader for the Toddlers.

Over the years Christ has transformed my mind and heart and has done what seemed impossible. I went from being someone who was bored, worried, in debt, loose morality, lack of purpose, and living for myself, to someone who lived with a purpose, active lifestyle, finally out of debt, serving, and finding the key to peace is living in Christ. It's incredible to me that after all I've done, the moral lows that I have hit in my life, that Christ has actually forgiven me, set me free, and I get to live this new life with Him leading and guiding along.

I finally went from believing there was a God, to understanding what it was to have a relationship with Christ. I began to pray and grow in my prayer life, and prayed for my family and friends so they could know what I now knew.

I've had the amazing experience of receiving His healing several times, being able to go on missions abroad and in Vancouver, being stretched way beyond what I would have challenged myself with on my own. In difficult times I can go to Him right away, and I'm part of a supportive community. The city that I at one point could have left and not made a single dent is now the city that I run into people I know everywhere I go, and is where I currently live out my purpose in Christ. I was just engaged to be married and finally am experiencing what it's like to be in a healthy Christian relationship.

Serving as a leader in the church led to having the privilege of working at Coastal Church for almost 8 years now. I would have never, ever guessed this is where my life would lead, but with Christ – anything's possible!

Jen Neuman serves as the Senior Administrator for our Strathcona Campus, and gives oversight and logistic planning to Coastal missions trips, event planning and benevolence.

Jen Neuman

Chapter 1

Coastal Story

I n Metro Vancouver, the majority of new churches that have succeeded are in the suburbs, while the high-rise community has struggled to establish a new church presence. Coastal Church faced numerous obstacles in growing from a fledgling church plant to where it is today—a contributor to the spiritual transformation of the City of Vancouver.

I did not consider myself to be the best qualified person for this project, yet God had seen fit to call me from a rural background and place me in the anchor block of the city. In 1992, I left a successful career in the oil industry to answer the call to pastor. Having grown up on a farm in Alberta, I gained a strong work ethic, which prepared me to take on the rigours of urban ministry. It was to our benefit that my wife, Cheryl, and I did not understand the scope of the challenge we would face. Others are drawn to the city for the urban lifestyle, but for us it was simply the empty faces and broken lives that moved us to tears and compelled us to ministry. When I asked the Lord why He would want me at this post, His response was: "Because you are not distracted."

In October of 1993, I led a group of Bible school students to witness on the streets of the West End of Vancouver. They were part of the World Harvest School of Ministry, which was an extension of Victory Christian Centre, now Relate Church, in Surrey, British Columbia. I was serving as the director of the Bible school, and as a staff pastor at this church. John Burns, the senior pastor, had taken me for a drive through this area of the city and explained the need for a spirit-filled church in the heart of the city.

In February of 1994, with the help of the Victory Christian Centre congregation, the church planting team conducted an extensive study in the downtown high-rise community of Vancouver, to understand the spiritual climate. At that time, we found only 3 percent were committed Christians. Our search to find a meeting space confirmed the anti-church attitude of the community–only one hotel would consider hosting us. At that time, there was just one other recent church plant downtown, plus the existing seven traditional churches which had served the community for decades.

After much prayer and preparation, an outreach service began on the night of Friday, April 15, 1994, at the Landmark Hotel on Robson Street. Throughout the spring and summer, church was held on Friday nights until enough of a core group was formed to begin Sunday services on September 11, 1994. This initial group of forty faithful believers was comprised of five members from my family, twenty-five new people who lived in the neighbourhood, and ten people who supported us from our sending church.

One of our mentors at that time encouraged us to stay connected to the church that was sending us out. Like every other church plant, the initial days required a significant amount of setting up and tearing down for each Sunday service, yet for the first year Cheryl and I, despite the fatigue, felt we must endeavor to be part of the Sunday evening services at Victory Christian Centre. As time has passed, the importance of that lesson from our mentor has paid huge dividends and impacted the stability of our lives and the church.

In the formative years of the church, the Board of Directors decided Coastal Church would be a non-denominational church. This decision came after prayer and consideration of the other options. Today, our church leadership feels that it has been a benefit in welcoming the urban dwellers from such varied religious and ethnic backgrounds. At the time, we were not aware of it but, there was a shift in Canada where people were choosing to be identified as a Christian and not a specific denomination. A 2001 census by Statistics Canada revealed "the number of people who declared themselves as [simply] "Christians"...skyrocketed 131 percent in British Columbia since 1991, to 200,000."[3]

There was little support from the church community in the early days because our new church plant did not fit the mold of a typical inner city work that focuses in poverty and addiction. For those who lived outside the downtown core, our church was seen as another inner city mission in the DTES. This area of the city, although only a few blocks from our location, faces great challenges with drug abuse, poverty, and homelessness. It has also received the most attention from numerous churches and non-profit organizations. Our mission field in the West End, was an entirely different world. It is densely populated with urban dwellers whose felt needs are much less obvious than those in the grip of poverty. It is our experience that there is less attention by the church community to reach these individuals.

Perhaps the greatest challenge in starting a work among towering buildings, where land is at a premium, was finding a place to meet. The community centre, which has a mandate to serve the various groups of the city, clearly told us that a church was not welcome on a regular basis. Usually schools are a good choice for a church to rent from, but we found a resistive group that simply did not want the stigma of a church meeting in their facilities. At just the right time God brought a young businessman into our lives who had recently rededicated his life to Christ. He was quite evasive about his background, but said he would help us find a place. Later we would discover his family was one of the prominent families in the city and was extremely well connected. He scouted the area for us and came back with only one hotel that was willing to allow us to meet on a weekly basis, the Landmark

Hotel. There was no mistaking that we were embarking on a spiritual battle for a city where the enemy had a stronghold for years.

In the spring of 1996, we saw, yet again, God's hand of provision for us. After months of renting in the hotel, we found a location owned by a multi-national company that was willing to lease us office property. There is limited public meeting space downtown, and most of it is overbooked. The company expected no problems with the City of Vancouver to allow us to use the space for assembly. We soon found out that we were facing the same forces of darkness we encountered when trying to rent in the hotels. Almost a year later, after hiring a consultant who was an expert in city zoning, we were finally given permission to move in.

In the process of finding venues to meet in, we learned some of the most valuable lessons that brought transformation to our lives. For example, one early lesson we learned was to buy used furniture and save money wherever it was possible, but to pay for the best lawyers, accountants, and consultants. We were coming to an understanding of Proverbs 15:22 which states, "plans go wrong for lack of advice; many counselors bring success" (NLT).

Unfortunately, the company we leased from had decided at this time to sell the building. Our initial response was disappointment after spending a year of hard work to make preparations for this location. In this situation, we were learning the importance of patiently trusting our Lord to provide. After giving this impossible situation to the Lord, the company called us back with a unique proposal. Although they could not provide a place for our congregation to meet, they did have an office building next-door, where they could rent us space for our office needs and to hold training meetings. The price was amazingly, only ten dollars per month! When we asked why, they responded that they understood that a church brings stability and wholeness to the community, and the city here was in need of it. We did find humor in the agreement. Although our office space cost was ten dollars per month, our parking stall included in the lease was one hundred dollars!

Another lesson we learned here was that the secular business community is watching how the church functions. If they see integrity and commitment they will often surprise one with unprecedented support. The bonus is they do not qualify someone on theology; they are just thankful someone is making a difference.

On this journey we discovered that the more commitment our church showed the city by investing in real estate or leasing property, the more commitment they showed us. Our neighbours were watching us closely to see if we were here for the long haul, or if this endeavour was just some kind of church experiment. In our area of the city there had been very few church plants that had a visible presence on the street. In fact, it had been over fifty years since a new church had acquired a church building in the core of the city.

The history of acquiring our building formed a key part in making the city of Vancouver a better place. Buildings speak of presence, influence and commitment. Thirty years ago there were few temples and mosques in Vancouver, but today as they spring up, it is obvious Muslims, Hindus, and other religions are impacting our city. God had placed a strong desire in our hearts to acquire a building to worship in. Little did we know He would position us on the new anchor block in the changing landscape of our city. This block has become the ceremonial street for major events such as parades, demonstrations, victory celebrations for sporting fans and marathon runs.

The First Church of Christ Scientist building was only a few blocks from where we met. Nearly a hundred years ago the teachings of Mary Baker Eddy were flourishing in the city. Since this congregation was left with only a dozen aging members, we approached them about the possibility of leasing the building to us. They insisted this was against the bylaws as set out by the headquarters of the church in Boston. On a summer's day in 1998 I sat down with another pastor on the steps of the building, and we asked the Lord for a plan of action in acquiring this strategic building.

It was two years later in the summer of 2000 that the building was listed for sale. This listing appeared in spite of the fact that we had specifically asked the board of The First Church of Christ Scientist to let us know if they ever decided to sell the building. Our hope was to avoid a bidding war with developers and save on realtor fees. There was little cooperation from this organization to help us and we found ourselves among giant developers looking to acquire this prime property.

In making the decisions that were necessary to move forward, we had to understand how to work with our Board of Directors and the congregation. During this time, I found the leadership material of John Maxwell inspirational. On the practical side, I studied the *Charities Handbook*[4] and *Serving as a Board Member*[5] that are provided by the Canadian Council of Christian Charities. One of the benefits of this struggling season was that it served to galvanize our church board and church family.

After sharing the vision in the year 2000 with the church about our desire to purchase the building for $3.5 million, I met with local business advisors to develop a plan to finance the purchase of the property. At the end of this intensive period of prayer and hard work, we did not have the financial backing to purchase the building. The realtor who handled the property expressly told us we would never own the building. He informed us it was too valuable for church use and suggested we move out to the suburbs like the rest of the churches and purchase a warehouse there. We battled discouragement at this time, since we had failed to raise the funds to buy the building. However, this setback had only increased our resolve in finding another way to acquire it.

The developer who purchased the property from the First Church of Christ Scientist was a devout Muslim whose company owned many of the five-star hotels in the area. He agreed to rent us the building until it was demolished. We now planned for our first service in the building on Easter Sunday on April 15, 2001. The business community saw the church as a positive thing and responded accordingly by assisting us in remodeling the interior of the building.

Over the next year we focused our energy on finding a way to purchase this property. There were numerous parties who also were pursuing this key location, including The City of Vancouver. The City desired to make a deal with the developer and use the facility as an arts and community centre. This felt like a chapter out of the book of Nehemiah, where Sanballat was taking another approach to intimidate us (Neh 6).

It was a year of great flux. We were always in a state of high alert as the battle for this little piece of land seemed to be intensifying and the number of interested parties began to circle it like vultures. A local nightclub with plenty of cash was knocking at the door trying to buy the building and convert the church into a nightclub. Our hearts were grieved, and we continued to cry out to God to have a presence in the city.

Over the course of the upcoming months, the church continued to pray even though there was little progress. In August of 2001, I brought in a real estate consultant with me to negotiate with the owner of the building. His skills prepared the way for us to make a deal with the owner and also assisted me in presenting our financial needs with a foundation sympathetic to church plants. By December, an agreement had been arranged for the foundation to loan us the money we required, interest free, for twenty years.

During this season of financial challenges, Wayne Myers, a missionary with Christ For The Nations in Dallas, Texas, spoke to our congregation. Wayne first entered Mexico to plant churches in 1946, and today he is the spiritual father to hundreds of pastors in that nation. He encouraged us to intentionally look for financial ways to help other churches around the world with their facility needs. His counsel was to obey what Jesus said in Luke 6:38, 'If you give, you will receive. Your gift will return to you in full measure, pressed down, shaken together to make room for more, and running over. Whatever measure you use in giving—large or small—it will be used to measure what is given back to you" (NLT). As a result, our church paid for a new church roof in the Philippines and raised the funds to purchase a building for a new church plant in Mexico.

In the midst of this battle for a new church presence in the city we were learning the importance of understanding how to negotiate for both leasing and acquiring property. In my experience, this area is one that church planters receive little or no training in, yet to succeed, the church planter must have a basic understanding of leasing and acquiring property. I acquired basic real estate knowledge by making numerous trips to the city library and by meeting with developers, who took time to teach me the fundamentals of zoning, property transfer, and structuring a financial plan.

It is vital that due diligence is done on the business side of things, but there is a spiritual realm that influences the decisions that are made. In our experience, we found that when the leaders of the church pray and fast about these difficult matters, the greatest progress is made.

In April of 2002 we had a major breakthrough as the developer agreed to sell the church building. To purchase the building at this point would now cost us an additional one million dollars. The turning point came when our consultant, who had grown up in Malaysia and understood the Islamic mindset, challenged the developer on whether he really wanted to be known as the man who tore down the church on Georgia Street. The next few months were incredibly intense for us, but by the grace of God, the deal was completed in August of that year.

Fast forward to today, we see that the current environment is inspiring a fresh interest in the church community to impact the city with the Gospel. In the downtown area there are several new church plants which have been established.

Along with the church planting initiative, there is also an increasing effort by the churches to work together. One area of need that is unifying churches is the increasing plight of homelessness in the city. Conferences are being held by church leaders to collaborate on making the city a better place. At these meetings different models are being studied that are producing results within Canada.

In the past twenty years there has also been a gradual shift in our community in the type of residents we have. The cost of housing has attracted residents in a higher income bracket who have a demand for quality living.[6] Income in our neighbourhood has increased 14 percent during the period between 2005 and 2008.[7] Next door to Coastal Church is the Shangri-La Hotel, which also has forty floors of residential units. This five-star hotel, along with a number of other such properties, has raised the level of expectation for quality of service in the neighbourhood. For a church to succeed in this community, it too must adapt and offer a level of hospitality residents are experiencing in the local stores, restaurants, and residential towers.

In order to keep up with the change we need to develop strategies to reach the current downtown community, and we review the demographics on a regular basis. This information for Canada is quite sobering. The last major census done for Canada in 2001 revealed that those who say they are Christians have been dropping by 1 percent a year. If this continues, by the year 2023 Christians will be outnumbered by non-Christians.[8]

The demographics for our community are typically divided into two districts, the West End and the Downtown Vancouver Business Improvement Area (BIA). In most sectors there is little difference between these two areas. The trends from the demographics influence the style of worship services and programs that we offer to the congregation. These categories include:

1) The population base and age of the residents.
   There are over seventy thousand people living in the community where our church is located. Of these residents, 50 percent are between the ages of twenty and thirty-nine.[9] Based on this demographic, decisions are made about

everything from style of music, decorating, length of service, the use of multi-media, and advertising.

2) The education level of the residents.

Those living in our community have a much higher level of education with 64 percent holding a university degree, compared to the rest of Metro Vancouver with 46 percent and only 8 percent having no secondary education[10]. This level of education has a direct affect on the type of courses that are run in the church, the way in which we follow up with people, and placing people into areas of service.

Figure 1 – Education Levels[11]

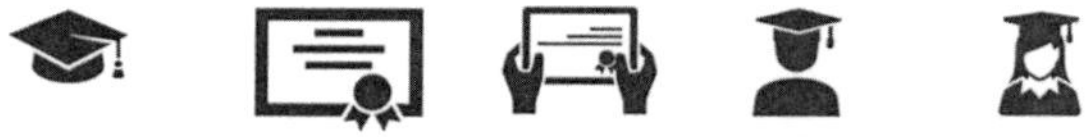

	NO CERTIFICATE, DIPLOMA, OR DEGREE	HIGH SCHOOL CERTIFICATE	TRADES CERTIFICATE OR DIPLOMA	COLLEGE OR OTHER NON-UNIVERSITY	UNIVERSITY
DOWNTOWN BIA	8%	22%	6%	18%	46%
VANCOUVER	17%	24%	6%	15%	39%
METRO VANCOUVER	17%	27%	9%	16%	31%

Population 15 Years or Older

3) The religious affiliation for Vancouver.

With approximately 41.5 percent of the population claiming to have no religion, and this statistic growing among the younger population, we see this as an opportunity to present the Gospel in a spiritual vacuum. These demographics also reveal the approach we need to focus on in reaching our community. For example, to reach those with no religion we found the Alpha Course to be successful in answering their questions and providing an environment where they can experience the power of the Holy Spirit. The distribution of the various religions in Vancouver is represented in the chart below.

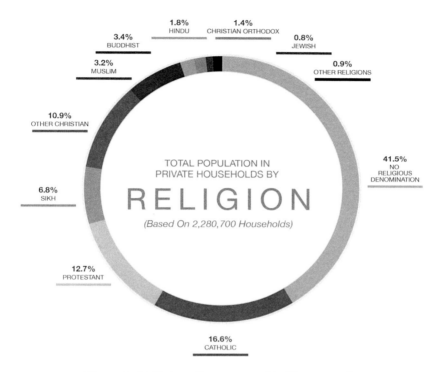

Figure 2. Religions Represented in Vancouver[10].

**NUMBER OF
HOUSEHOLDS**

49,546
DOWNTOWN BIA

253,215
VANCOUVER

817,030
METRO VANCOUVER

**AVERAGE
NUMBER OF
PERSONS/
HOUSEHOLD**

1.6
DOWNTOWN BIA

2.2
VANCOUVER

2.6
METRO VANCOUVER

**PERCENT OF
HOUSEHOLDS
WITH FAMILIES**

32%
DOWNTOWN BIA

58%
VANCOUVER

71%
METRO VANCOUVER

**NUMBER OF
FAMILIES**

15,725
DOWNTOWN BIA

145,605
VANCOUVER

580,120
METRO VANCOUVER

**AVERAGE
NUMBER OF
PERSONS/
FAMILY**

2.4
DOWNTOWN BIA

2.9
VANCOUVER

3.0
METRO VANCOUVER

**AVERAGE
NUMBER OF
CHILDREN/
FAMILY**

0.5
DOWNTOWN BIA

1.0
VANCOUVER

1.1
METRO VANCOUVER

Table 1. Family Structure in Vancouver[11].

4) The unique family structure of the downtown core.
   Households with families comprise only 32 percent in
   the downtown core, compared with 71 percent in Metro
   Vancouver. In this environment, we respond with teaching
   and programs that deal with the challenges for the singles in our community. For those who do have children,
   they find very little support, so by offering services to
   the family, they find the church to be an oasis. One service that has been very beneficial to the community is a
   licensed Coastal Preschool program, which runs daily in
   the building.

5) The ratio of men to women in the Vancouver West End
   Here we find a male population of 56 percent.[14] This ratio
   is primarily due to the concentration of the gay community. As a result, our church has to proactively respond
   with a men's ministry that promotes healthy relationships
   and biblical family values. Issues such as sexuality, divorce,
   addiction, suicide, and loneliness need to be addressed.

6) The cost of housing.
   Our neighbourhood is an expensive area to live in, with
   the average apartment selling for just over $600 thou-
   sand.[15] In this densely populated area, 98 percent of the
   residents live in apartments.[16] The income over the years
   has not matched the rising cost of housing in Vancouver.
   These factors influence things such as the way we approach
   doing our Life Groups to conducting seminars on personal finances.

7) The income and employment patterns.
   The average household income is close to fifty thousand
   dollars.[17] The study conducted by First Baptist Church
   revealed, "the dominant occupation categories are: Sales
   and Service (23%); Business, Finance & Administration
   (21%); Management (15%)." [18]

8) The ethnic origin and language.

On any given Sunday there are over sixty different nationalities represented in our services. This diversity is a mirror image of the community we live in, yet for 60 percent of our community, English is the primary language with Chinese a distant second.[19] The graph below illustrates this mosaic of Vancouver as reported in the 2006 census of ethnic origins by Statistics Canada[20]. By understanding the dynamics of the culture and ethnic groups around us, we are better equipped to serve them. As mentioned earlier we hire staff accordingly, translate services into the most needed languages, advertise in certain ethnic papers, and purpose to keep our love for Christ the common bond between us.

Figure 3 - Vancouver Ethnic Origin Distribution

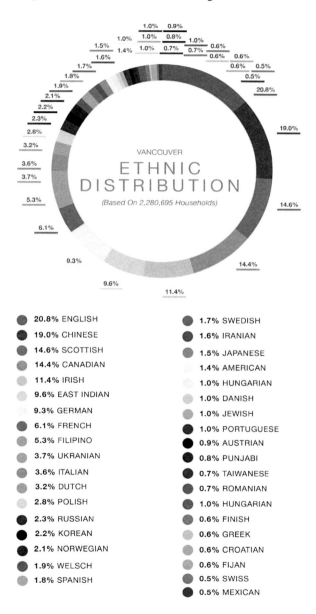

20.8% ENGLISH	1.7% SWEDISH
19.0% CHINESE	1.6% IRANIAN
14.6% SCOTTISH	1.5% JAPANESE
14.4% CANADIAN	1.4% AMERICAN
11.4% IRISH	1.0% HUNGARIAN
9.6% EAST INDIAN	1.0% DANISH
9.3% GERMAN	1.0% JEWISH
6.1% FRENCH	1.0% PORTUGUESE
5.3% FILIPINO	0.9% AUSTRIAN
3.7% UKRANIAN	0.8% PUNJABI
3.6% ITALIAN	0.7% TAIWANESE
3.2% DUTCH	0.7% ROMANIAN
2.8% POLISH	1.0% HUNGARIAN
2.3% RUSSIAN	0.6% FINISH
2.2% KOREAN	0.6% GREEK
2.1% NORWEGIAN	0.6% CROATIAN
1.9% WELSCH	0.6% FIJAN
1.8% SPANISH	0.5% SWISS
	0.5% MEXICAN

We can conclude that the downtown core of Vancouver will continue to be a changing landscape. In order for us to bring a transformation into this environment, Coastal Church will have to persist in monitoring the trends and adapting accordingly. If we hope to see a reversal in the declining Christian population in our city, the church community will need to aggressively plant more congregations here. In order for this endeavour to take place, called leaders must be trained up, and funding must be provided. Strategies are required to communicate this vision with those who can financially support new ventures. Proverbs 29:18a says, "Where there is no vision, the people will perish" (KJV). The demographics of our city will only change as we continue to look at the harvest the way Christ instructed us to.

Fari's Story

Born in the Islamic Republic of Iran on September 2, 1981, I was brought up as a Muslim believer. I was taught to pray five times a day, attended Mosque services, and memorized passages from the Quran to recite in school. That was the only religion I knew then, and I had actually never heard about the person called Jesus. Then my family and I moved to Denmark when I was 11 years old. It was a big change, however an important one. Even though Denmark is called a Christian country, I was never introduced to Christianity. We only attended church for different holiday events or when our school took us on field trips. However, my knowledge of God was all about to change after my mom, sister and I moved to Canada in 2000.

After a few years of living in Vancouver, I worked as a Personal Trainer for Shirley Seto at a gym, whom I later introduced to my mom, Ashley. A great friendship started between Shirley and my mom, which was slowly cultivated. It was during this time that my mom was searching for something to bring her peace and answers to the tough questions of life. Shirley, sensitive to this, invited my mom to the church she attended, Coastal Church.

This was my mom's first time in her fifty years to step into a church and hear the Good News. This would also be the day where my mom was drawn by God's loving-kindness to repentance and to receive a new birth through faith in Jesus Christ.

After such an encounter with God, my mom started to share the Gospel with me and my sister Hasti, which became our introduction to Christianity and who Jesus is. Hasti and I did not believe in Jesus at once. I can't explain why and how I finally decided to attend church and look into the story of Jesus for myself. Now, I know today that it was because I had a mom praying and fasting along with her Persian life group at Coastal Church for at least a year and half until Hasti and I gave our lives to Christ. I am forever grateful for my mom's perseverance in sharing the Gospel with both of us and praying without ceasing.

When I began attending Coastal Church, the church services seemed strange to me and I was out of my comfort zone. Coming from a Muslim background, I only knew religion from what I had seen and experienced in Mosques and the streets of Iran. However, after my eyes were opened to the truth of the Gospel and I felt the love of Christ through the church, I got to see the value and the necessity of attending church and pursuing Jesus.

I accepted Jesus Christ as my Lord and Saviour and decided to be water baptized by Pastor Dave Koop on April 25, 2004 at English Bay. I clearly remember that my life started to change drastically after my public declaration of my faith and devotion to Jesus Christ. Since I was new to the faith and had to learn what it meant to be a follower of Christ, I was spiritually immature and had a hard time committing every area of my life to God. Amongst such struggles, I was grateful to be a part of a community who loved Christ and were living to know Him more every day. I was connected to a great life group and started to learn more about Jesus and my new identity in Christ. At this time in my journey of faith I was very focused on health, fitness and my career. There were many hurts and habits in my life that I needed freedom and healing from. Slowly, but surely the Spirit of God started to mold, correct, convict and encourage me to consistently seek His Kingdom and righteousness.

In 2005, God started revealing His will for my life and the call to full-time ministry. On a Sunday morning Pastor Anthony

Greco from Calgary Life Church was the special guest speaker invited to share the message, as Pastor Dave was in China for his Doctor of Ministry studies. By the end of the service which I was attending, Pastor Anthony came forward, prayed and prophesied over me telling me what was already put in my heart by God. He explained to me that God wanted me to change my lifestyle and put all fleshly things aside and start seeking Him with all my heart. His plan for me was and is to be a fellow worker in spreading the Gospel of Jesus Christ. That summer I decided to enrol in full-time studies at Christ for The Nations Bible College. After three years I received my Bachelor of Theology in Pastoral Leadership, through the grace of God and the great patience and love of the staff at the college. Since then through His grace I have grown spiritually in love, holiness and in the saving knowledge of Jesus Christ.

In 2006 after having known each other for about a year and a half, Angela and I became husband and wife and started our journey towards growing in Christlikeness and serving God together. Today we have two beautiful girls who are truly a gift from God.

God has given me amazing opportunities through Coastal Church. I was able to complete my internship under Pastor Dave & Cheryl Koop where I acquired more knowledge about God, ministry and leadership. Angela and I also had the chance to work with Coastal youth for about 4 years and we saw God move mightily in the lives of the youth and in multiplying the number of youth attending church today.

In 2008, after graduating at Bible College I started working full-time as an Outreach Worker at the Union Gospel Mission, a ministry that brings restoration to those in poverty and addiction in Vancouver downtown eastside. God has taught me many life lessons through the guests that come into the Mission and from awesome godly staff that I served with during that time.

On January 7, 2014 I stepped into the role of a campus Pastor for Coastal Church's third site at Strathcona in Downtown East

Side. It has been an amazing experience of starting a new campus in a community where I have already served the people for about 6 years. There have been challenges and obstacles but God has never failed us and He continues to empower and guide us. I feel extremely privileged to be able to be a part of building and expanding God's Kingdom. I have succeeded in many tasks and failed in others, however, God has always been there to pick me up and to guide me forward. At this time, I am also enrolled at Carey Theological College working towards my Master of Divinity and I am very grateful for my teachers and fellow students there.

I can truthfully say today that I have the peace and satisfaction that I have never experienced before surrendering my life to Christ. I have a passion to win souls for God's kingdom and to push back the kingdom of darkness that is keeping many in bondage. I know the purpose of my being and who I am supposed to become; I am the light and the salt of the earth, a child of God, a slave of righteousness, a son of God, a temple of God, a member of Christ's body, an heir of God and one in Christ, a saint, a prisoner of Christ, a royal priesthood, and I am born of God and for God. And I give all praise to Jesus Christ my God and Saviour who paid a great price for me and for whosoever calls on His name.

Fari Ghaem-Maghami serves as an assistant pastor at Coastal Church overseeing the Strathcona Campus in the Vancouver Downtown Eastside. Fari and Angela are parents to two girls Abreena and Layla.

Fari & Angie Ghaem-Maghami.

Chapter 2

Keys to Impacting Our City

The downtown core of Vancouver has attracted attention from city planners around the world. It is one of the most densely populated areas in North America, with close to seventy thousand people living in less than one square mile. "The entire downtown peninsula currently employs almost 145,000 people."[21] The city has intentionally worked hard to attract people back into the city core, where they live, work, play, and do life together. Tragically, the influence of the church in this transformation has been barely visible. Into this environment, Coastal Church was planted in 1994. By God's grace the church took root – despite my wife's and my lack of training and resources.

To plant a church in an urban setting takes a certain amount of courage and raw faith. Added to that, a global perspective is required to benefit from the wisdom of successful ministries in cities around the world. It also requires an understanding of, and an ongoing adjustment to, the changes that take place in the church's neighborhood. For example, next door to the church there used to stand a derelict nightclub, but today a five-star hotel and high-end retail store occupy this space.

From day one, it has been a steep learning curve to identify the next steps needed for sustainable growth. But by the grace of

God we have seen consistent growth in our church attendance and water baptisms.

Figure 4 – Coastal Church Weekend Attendance

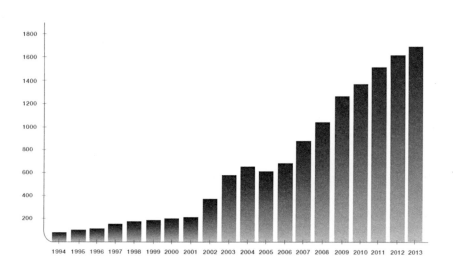

Figure 5 – Coastal Church Water Baptisms

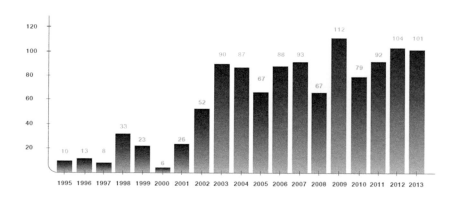

Over the past twenty years we discovered some key strategies that have proven to work in a changing environment:

1. Engage our City through Personal Relationships

It all started when we embarked on an extensive telephone campaign. In February 1994, over a period of thirty days we worked with the Bible school that sent us out to methodically go through a directory, and call over thirty thousand residents of the downtown core of Vancouver. Our church planting team personally made contact with over ten thousand people. We sent a mail-out to the majority of those we connected with, announcing the launch of the new church plant.

Early in the campaign, after conducting what was called a "1,000 dial up test," the consultants for the project informed us we were in a "highly resistive area" however, based on their results in other cities, they encouraged us with their estimation that we would have between two hundred and four hundred people at the first meeting. The first meeting on April 15, 1994 resulted in only four new people coming as a result of this massive undertaking. It was a disappointment, but nonetheless, we learned a valuable lesson early on that this type of impersonal approach would not work in our community.

The strategy of going on the street and handing out tracts was also unproductive. We soon learned that in the core of our city we had three main groups of people:

a) The residents, who were our main target. We found they were the most resistive to any type of aggressive evangelism.

b) Those that commuted to the core of the city to work or for recreation. These people tolerated being approached, but since it was not their community, they really did not care.

c) Tourists visiting the city who were perhaps the most open, but would never be part of our local church.

In an attempt to be more personal we introduced the "Jesus Video Campaign" promoted by Campus Crusade for Christ. Since this outreach program had achieved great results around the world, the church leadership felt it would be a good fit for us. Today their website claims, "no other film has been seen by more than 4.9 billion people, translated into 766 languages, and shown in 236 countries."[22] It was another large investment for us, both in finances and in volunteer hours. In the Fall of 1994, the approach was to follow up on the names of any contacts we had in the community. We made contact with these individuals and delivered the videos with a highly personal touch. After a month of following the prescribed follow up plan we saw no growth in the church.

From these outreach experiments we learned several valuable lessons:

    a) People in our community were looking for sincere relationships before presenting them with the Gospel message, no matter how well it was packaged.

    b) The residents of Vancouver would be suspicious of anything that came across like a sales or marketing pitch. They were looking for something more authentic; they did not want to feel like they were being coerced into or even badgered into coming to church.

What we did find to work amazingly well was the "Alpha" course birthed out of Holy Trinity Brompton Church, located in South Kensington, London, England. We began this course in 1996 when new believers expressed to us that they needed a greater understanding of the basic questions about Christianity. The first time we used the course, the entire church went though the material. The lessons were taught on Sunday, and then each small group discussed the topics in their homes. We discovered the "Alpha" course served a twofold purpose for us. First, it served to provide a foundation for the new believers and for those who were returning to church. Secondly, we were pleasantly surprised that it developed into an environment that newcomers came to faith in Christ.

Some factors that we found to contribute to the success of the "Alpha" course were:

a) The training available for the team was practical and well laid out.

b) The course was led by volunteers rather than the church pastors, resulting in attendees feeling more relaxed.

c) The mealtime cultivated a place for people to build relationships.

d) The high level of excellence in everything from the food to the venue attracted the urban condo dwellers.

e) Intentionally choosing leaders that have a good sense of humour also added to the positive experience of the participants.

f) Having small groups where leaders only facilitated the conversation helped people feel free to express themselves. No one was allowed to preach or give the right answer to every question. Rather, each table was designed to be a place where everyone could share their opinions.

g) The fact that the course was British, and that it came out of an Anglican church seemed to add credibility. Canadians, as members of the British Commonwealth, feel an affinity to teachers and ministers from this background.

h) The talks given by Reverend Nicky Gumbel were skillfully communicated.

2. Provide a Place to Do Life – Community

The popular television series of the 1980s, "Cheers", had a theme song that captures the mood of citified life. The lyrics still ring out in cities today: "Sometimes you want to go where everybody knows your name, and they're always glad you came. You want to be where you can see; our troubles are all the same. You wanna be where everybody knows your name. You wanna go where people know, people are all the same, you wanna go where everybody knows your name."[23]

Over the past years, those living in Vancouver have seen the city planners encourage the development of the available lands into high-rise commercial or residential property. With the increase in density, locations for city dwellers to do life together in a community have diminished. Living in a 500 square foot apartment only amplifies the need for social interaction. In this setting, the church has so much to offer as a place to go where people do know their names, and the troubles are all the same. In response to this cry, as a church we are constantly looking for fresh ways to promote community. Connecting once a week on Sunday is not sufficient to build meaningful relationships. In response, we endeavor to use the building as a tool on a daily basis providing outlets that include all ages, from a Preschool, an annual Urban Kid's Camp, Youth groups, to Young Adult events. The more we do life with the residents of our city, the more they understand that we are authentic. With each step we have taken to increase our commitment, the community has responded in kind. For example, after renting our first office space, Sunday attendance increased. When we purchased and restored a building, the response was an additional increase in attendance.

3. Utilize Small Groups

The single biggest issue in the urban center, despite the dense population, is loneliness. Approximately 58 percent of Vancouverites live alone in the community with the average number of people per household being 2.2.[24] This sense of isolation was recognized when we first began to hold our church services in a hotel breakout room. From there we began small group settings, which struck a chord with those who were coming, and soon they were inviting their friends. Finally, we began to see an increase in our attendance. We learned whatever we could from the Cell Group Movement and tweaked it for our context. For example, compared to other suburban churches, our groups were typically smaller due to the restricted apartment living space.

We discovered that compared to other settings, it took longer to see a small group multiply in the downtown setting of our city. Our church's research indicated that other communities were multiplying small groups within six months, while our groups were taking over a year to reach this point. We felt one of the reasons for this was that people in the high-rise community are typically more guarded and trust is established slowly. This mistrust is evident with apartments having buzzer numbers, elevator swipes, and alarm systems.

As people began to trust each other, the groups began to grow organically. Trying to put everything in neat boxes and flowcharts proved futile and frustrating. When our church attempted to place people strictly by location or age, it backfired. After a period of trial and error we learned to empower the groups to form around the common interests they had, yet at the same time to keep the groups moving forward in a unified manner by reviewing and discussing the weekly sermon. People bonded when they were encouraged to truly do life together the way they saw fit in the heart of the city, while keeping Christ as the focal point.

4. Promote Family

Promoting a sense of family and belonging, despite what the demographics reveal, is another key to impacting the community. In 2003, our church participated in a community study conducted by Vancouver's First Baptist Church that confirmed what we had come to understand. This was an area with very few children and married couples. This study revealed that only 6 percent of the population in this area is under that age of nineteen and only 24 percent are married.[25] In our community, about 60 percent of the population lives alone. In this setting, we discovered that people are drawn to the stability and security of a functioning family.

This desire to connect is especially true for the immigrants who tend to cluster where a familial network can be established. When they discover a setting that promotes traditional family structure and values, they soon invite others from their backgrounds to the church. The church becomes the community centre in a new land.

For the singles in our community, the church provides an environment for them to connect and interact with family life that might not otherwise be available to them. Here there is an opportunity to volunteer in the children's ministry, or to visit an aging grandparent. Those with families will typically invite a number of singles over for Christmas and other festive occasions. As a result, these individuals feel the warmth of family, and furthermore they feel a sense of belonging.

My wife, Cheryl, and I struggled with bringing our children into the downtown environment. For Cheryl, it was especially challenging to give up the programs for children that are offered in the established suburban churches. We were concerned at times about the darker aspects of inner city life that our children were often exposed to. In urban areas children are often exposed to the realities of poverty, homelessness, and visible effects of drugs. We seriously wrestled with raising a family where we often had to explain behavior that was crude and offensive, yet we discovered that this exposure gave us an opportunity to have an open dialogue with our children, especially as they came into their teenage years. It served to strengthen their characters and help give them a world perspective.

5. Reach the Professionals

Downtown Vancouver residents have a higher level of education than average for the city and region, with 64 percent holding a university degree or diploma, as compared to 54 percent for Vancouver and 47 percent from Metro Vancouver overall.[26] Recent development projects are specifically designed for people to live and work in the same tower. The first thing we learned is to grant professionals plenty of time to investigate the philosophy of the church, its values, direction, and core beliefs. We find they want to belong, but they are cautious to affirm they are a member of the church until they have done their due diligence.

We found professionals tend to dress down on Sundays, and many times we have underestimated the influence of someone attending based on their clothing. The well-educated and savvy downtown resident will usually take the back row and watch for about a year before they make a move to be involved in the church. Those that intentionally come in late and leave early were nicknamed the "bolters." For most living in a culture that has a very caustic attitude about church, they simply want to test the water to see if it is real. Some stay on the fringe because of their previous religious experience. This fact was especially true of the Muslim community. Out of curiosity they would attend as a result of a friend's invitation to investigate what the "god of Canada" was like. Only after a lengthy period of observing us would they venture in closer to explore the claims of Christ.

6. Take an Uncompromising Approach to Biblical Truths

Coastal Church is located in the midst of British Columbia's new high-end retail, residential and business district. Our church building is anchored just next to the prestigious Shangri-La Hotel, and few other chic, luxurious brand stores such as Tiffany & Co., and Burberry.

Like every world-class city, behind such a façade of success and opulence lie layers of corruption, brokenness, and immorality. It is in this culture the church must learn to be relevant, while holding to the eternal truths of Scripture. In the church world there is always a "flavour of the month" or some "pet doctrine" that is overemphasized. As a church, we learned it is best to avoid extremes. Psalm 23 refers to the Lord leading beside still waters and green pastures. This type of an oasis needs to be a reality in the heart of a bustling city centre.

Our experience found that this "tribe" of urban dwellers would push away from extreme religious experiences. They are looking for stability and a tranquil sanctuary from the manic pace around them. When we moved into our church building with its pews from the turn of the twentieth century, some well meaning leaders and church growth "experts" informed us that this furniture would turn off the younger urbanite dwellers. We found the opposite to be true. The medium age of the church is thirty-three, and they are drawn to a setting that feels safe. Many of them are "first generation Christians," with little understanding of church, and to them the old building represented what they thought church was. They saw the art, the history, and applauded us for preserving a heritage building in the city.

We discovered the urbanized followers of Christ do not want a diluted version of the Gospel. Everything around the city resident screams bold, from the architecture of the buildings, art and commerce, to the hockey team that plays down the street. They want the uncompromised word of God even when it upsets them. They are saying: "Please communicate the message in my language: I am urban, I live in a world of trends, arts, and I am under great pressure to perform. I am technically savvy; I am on the move and my listening span is about thirty-five minutes." The key is to make it plain so they can understand it. As Paul states,

"Even though I am free of the demands and expectations of everyone, I have voluntarily become a servant to any and all in order to reach a wide range of people: religious, nonreligious, meticulous moralists, loose-living immoralists, the defeated, the demoralized—whoever. I didn't take on their way of life. I kept my bearings in Christ—but I entered their world and tried to experience things from their point of view. I've become just about every sort of servant there is in my attempts to lead those I meet into a God-saved life" (1 Cor. 9:19-23 MSG).

7. Celebrate the Arts

The Arts, no matter what the expression, is a powerful tool in preserving the message of the Gospel. Every generation looks for an avenue to showcase their creativity and for a community to support them. The church provides an environment that is both welcoming and forgiving. We have found that cultivating and celebrating the arts is somewhat challenging and yet at the same time very rewarding. It is necessary to lay down boundaries and encourage discipline when working with volunteer artists who can be quite fickle. For the up and coming Christian artist, there is a challenge with expressing his or her faith alongside contemporaries who do not share the same views. Steve Turner, in his book *A Vision for Christians in the Arts*, writes that these artists "are usually frustrated that there is so little distinctive Christian content in the contemporary arts, but on the other hand, they are embarrassed at the low standards of much of what is promoted as 'Christian art.'"[27] Our response in the church is to help raise the standard of the art and to encourage artists to use the gifts that God has given them to reach out to their friends. This approach has worked with some success with our musicians. The skills that they have in music have been honed here, and these musicians are playing at various social gatherings in the city. As a result, they have extended invitations for others to attend church and experience the love of God they have experienced.

The reward comes in observing confidence rise up in the artist as their gifts blossom. These young talented artists have gifts that communicate the Gospel in fresh ways and add a wonderful dimension of community. An example of this took place during one of our Police Appreciation Sundays. Brad, a young rap artist, who came out of a troubled background, performed a special song for the occasion. The police officers in attendance were deeply moved to see this young person off the street communicating the power of God's love through his artistic impression. A number of officers stated that this performance was the highlight of the event for them.

In the heart of the city, I discovered a wealth of artists in a variety of expressions. One of the events that unearthed this treasure was our summer camp for the children. As an urban church where the building takes up the entire footprint of the property, we do not have the space for the typical summer kids programs. We have no room for a soccer game or a basketball hoop, so it led us to review what we have. In taking inventory, we looked to the kitchen and asked some of our chefs with culinary skills to teach the children. Parents were invited for lunch and were shocked to be served chicken cordon bleu and crème brûlée for dessert. Within the church we found choreographers who celebrated the art of dance. Children arrived excited to learn dance moves from the same teacher that has worked professionally with well known Hollywood artists. Young students picked up a paintbrush, and under the instruction of one of the teachers from Emily Carr University of Art and Design, expressed themselves on canvas. The classes took their breaks together, and during this time the teachers wove in the lessons found in traditional vacation Bible school material.

8. Become Intentionally Multicultural

It is Coastal Church's position that the congregation should be a reflection of the people who dwell in the surrounding community. Often, the initial comment from visitors to our region of the city refers to their observation to the number of different nationalities who are represented. A nearby Starbucks welcome sign reflects this with a dozen languages posted on their front door, yet, just because a diverse population exists around one, it does not mean they will gravitate to the church.

People come to church for a variety of reasons. For the year 2012, we gathered and quantified the completed church Response Cards, which has a section for visitors to indicate how they came to church. Based on the analysis of Response Cards, which guests and members fill out weekly, most of them come to church as a result of a friend or relative's invitation. These results lead us to the conclusion that these guests are asking an important question: "Are there people here like me?" Even for those who have built up the courage to cross the church threshold after walking by the building or discovered the church on the Internet, this question is still foremost in their minds.

Figure 6 - How people found and came to Coastal Church

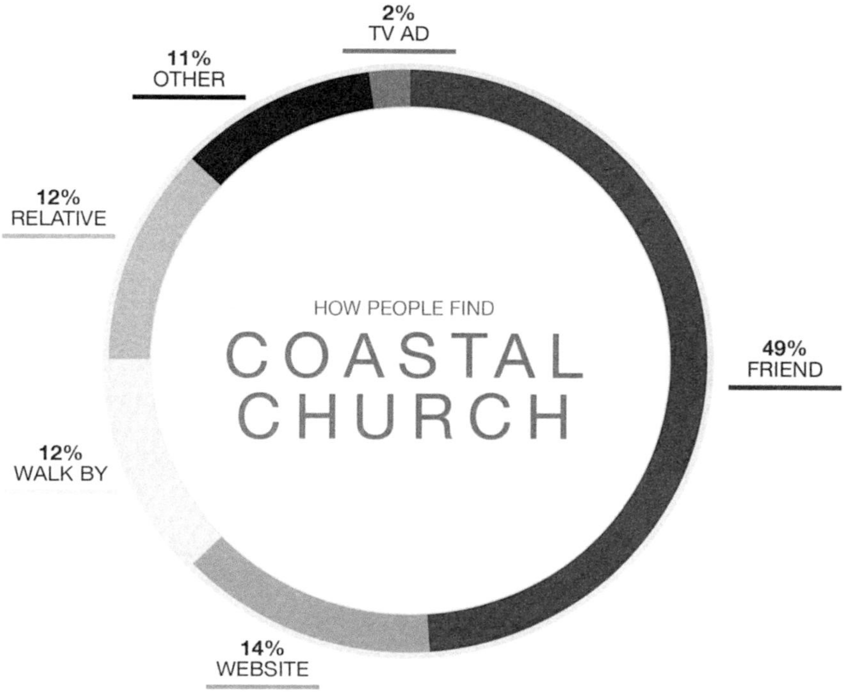

To help welcome people, we intentionally ensure that the volunteers, and especially the greeters, reflect the diverse ethnicities represented in the congregation. We have also found that it is important to display diversity on the stage. The stage is an area that people focus on to see if the church lives out what they believe about including various nationalities. It is important that the guests see that those who are ministering in song and the spoken word reflect the international flavour of our church and community.

On numerous occasions, we have been approached to conduct separate services for a certain nationality. This approach is common among the Korean, Filipino, and Persian communities in our city. The strategy we have used is to encourage them to meet in small groups and enjoy their language, food, and customs in that setting. For the congregational setting we are insistent that we all meet together. We all go to university, the grocery store, and the coffee shops together, so our approach has been not to segregate on a Sunday. The new immigrants to the country typically prefer to meet in a church that has their culture and language, but their children being the second generation immigrant, want to be "Canadian" and meet with everyone else.

Since many of our members do not have English as a first language, we endeavor to remove communication barriers. A simple, but effective tool has been to hand out detailed notes to be used in following the delivery of the sermon. This is useful because most of them will read English and have something to take home and study, before understanding it orally. The notes that are handed out are also used by the congregation when they listen to the message again over the Internet or via podcast.

Another strategy has been to translate the message in another language on an FM signal. This translation is accomplished by having a bilingual volunteer set up in a church office with a simple short range FM transmitter. As they hear the service in English, they translate the message into another language for those listening in the service with an FM headset. Those in the service can then sit with the other members but discreetly listen to the service in their own language. To date we have found this to work best for Spanish-speaking members. It has been interesting to observe that some nationalities welcome this service, while others decline the service, seeing it as an opportunity to learn English.

We also found it is important to train our volunteers to introduce newcomers to a small group leader who speaks their language. If this connection can take place in their first few visits, the newcomer soon finds that he or she fits in.

9. Keep the Church a House of Prayer

As the head of the church, Jesus clearly said that "[His] house shall be called a house of prayer" (Matt. 21:13 NIV).Therefore, if the church is to bring a transformation into any culture, it should be known as a place of prayer. The year we moved into our church facility, we received numerous offers from the movie industry offering large sums of money to rent the building to be used as a movie set. The prevailing attitude was that churches need money, and since they had the latest Hollywood star, we should allow them to set up shop. In this season the Lord spoke strongly to us that if we would consecrate the building for His glory, He would be our Provider.

We have found that dedicating ourselves and our building to prayer was essential for urban transformation. As Paul wrote in Ephesians 6:12: "For we do not wrestle against flesh and blood, but against principalities, against powers, against the rulers of the darkness of this age, against spiritual hosts of wickedness in the heavenly places." I appreciated Ralph Neighbour's comment in "How to Create an Urban Strategy": "Let those who are spiritually blind to eternal warfare stay away from developing urban strategy."[28] The spiritual realm should recognize Coastal Church is praying, and then by doing so the residents around us should sense a difference. The church will only survive and begin to transform a community if it initiates a specific prayer strategy. Everyone in the church will not understand the resulting spiritual battle, but the church leadership must be prepared to lead the way.

Coastal Church has grown its roots in the downtown core where God has continued to give us a love for the community. He has opened our eyes to the spiritual needs in a community that might be overlooked and as people seen to be overly successful or disinterested in spiritual matters. Without a doubt, being part of the downtown community over the years has taught us to contextualize church making it relevant to reach the unchurched, lonely, and broken generation of an urban centre. Whether conversing with someone in our residential building elevator; opening our church to the community; fostering friendship in small groups; preaching the full Gospel relevantly; promoting the arts; serving young families; embracing different cultures and stirring an attitude of prayer in the congregation, our church continues to seek strategies passionately to lead people to Jesus, making the City of Vancouver a better place.

Rob's Story

I emigrated from Scotland to Canada in 1967. I was 8 years old. My mother, one sister and 5 brothers, including myself, traveled by boat for 7 days and landed in Montreal, Canada. My father had come ahead of us and was working in Montreal. His job was to make blueprints to build boats. We lived in Montreal for 3 years and then moved to another city. Soon after we moved, my mother got sick and died. I had been a "momma's boy" and was very hurt when she died. My father was an alcoholic. He could not take care of us. My brothers and sisters tried to take care of me, but they couldn't because I was too angry over the loss of my mother.

I soon found out that alcohol and drugs were very soothing and a good way to hide my pain. I ended up in and out of juvenile detention homes from the time I was 12 until I was 16 years old. From there I went to jail. It became like a home to me because I knew everyone in there.

One day the police picked me up and told me if I didn't go to the other end of the country, they would keep on putting me in jail. They said they would let me out in the morning if I would get on the highway and go west, to Vancouver, and not come back.

In Vancouver, I continued selling drugs, drinking, living on the streets, going to jail, working on the carnival. I met a girl when I was on the carnival and she wanted to live with me so we could share the rent. I agreed, but we soon became parents and we knew nothing about how to be parents because I had no parents from the time I was 12.

I became a window cleaner and was good at my job. I was able to get a car and we began to socialize and party together. There were drugs at the parties and the girl I lived with, the mother of my 2 children, got hooked on drugs and that began a miserable life of living with someone that was abusive to me. I ended up living on the streets again to get away from the abuse, although I still had my job and car. I would take the children on the weekends, but the only problem was I was living in a tent and it wasn't a very good place for the children to stay.

One day, taking the children home after a weekend, I was drunk and hit a big truck with my car and almost killed my son and daughter. I would have to walk from my tent to the hospital to visit them every day, which were about 7 miles one way and then another 7 miles home. I was so hurting and frustrated that I went to the bar to get drunk and instead of asking for a beer, I asked for a coffee. I have never touched drugs or alcohol from that day on, which is now 26 years. The children eventually got out of the hospital. Three months later their mother came to take the children home, but she was high on crack cocaine. I said, "No, come back another day". I ended up gaining custody of the children and raising them by myself.

Nine years later, I met someone who invited me to a church banquet. I went and heard a man give his testimony about how Jesus had changed his life. I really identified with his testimony and I thought, "If God can change his life, maybe He could do the same for me".

I said to God "I believe you're there, but I need to know". God began to show me that He cared for me. On one occasion, I was spared from being hit by a train and I attributed that to God. My son and I hitch hiked across Canada to see my brother, who had come from Scotland. My son had attended a kids program at a local church and finally said to me "Dad, I've been praying for a ride and you keep turning them down". So I said, "Okay, let's pray and if we get a ride all the way to Montreal, when we get back to Vancouver, we're going to church". Sure enough, as God would have it, 5 minutes after we prayed, a van stopped and asked us if we wanted a ride-all the way to Montreal! Yes, and when we got home, I kept my word and went to church, Coastal of course.

The first service I attended was a very emotional experience for me. I had attended the Salvation Army church as a very young lad in Scotland and occasionally in Montreal, but all that ended when my mom died. As the worship began that morning, I had a big lump in my throat and found myself fighting to hold back the tears. I knew I was being touched by God. I didn't really know how to conduct myself in church, but I felt my apprehensions begin to leave, as people were singing and clapping and enjoying themselves, so I joined in. Then as Pastor Dave began to preach, it was as if he was talking to me. I had come with a lot of questions and even on that first sermon, he was addressing my concerns. I found myself thinking, "I've found my home".

Soon after that, I asked Jesus to come into my heart and forgive me of all my sins and make me clean with His blood. I began to change and everyone around me noticed the difference. I started to look different on the outside because I was changing on the inside. I loved coming to church and hearing about the Bible and I began to apply it to my life. I began going to Alpha and loved it so much I did it about 7 times. I met some amazing people and they are still my friends today. It was great being a part of a community of believers that welcomed me into their family. My church family was really the only family I had and I loved doing life with them. It was during the Alpha Holy Spirit weekend that I was filled with the Holy Spirit. I also learned at Alpha that Jesus heals today just as he did in Bible days. I had really messed up my neck in the car accident mentioned earlier and I could hardly move it. I approached my Life Group and asked them to pray for my neck. As they were praying, I heard a loud "ping" and felt my neck release. God healed me then and it has not bothered me since.

I had gone to Alcoholics Anonymous (AA) for many years and it did help me a lot, but it didn't address the spiritual part of my recovery. I approached Pastor Dave and asked if there was any way we could have a Christ centered step program in the church. Pastor began to research the possibilities and we started "Celebrate Recovery." I went through this 12 step program, and later on became involved as a facilitator and sponsor. Still to this day I love that I am able to continue my 12th step, through another similar program called "Freedom Session", by helping others find freedom from their hurts, hang-ups and habits and give back out of what I have learned.

I look back on my life now and it seems to be a dream. I can't imagine how I could have been like that. I am not the same person I used to be. 2 Corinthians 5:17 truly describes my life "Old things have passed away and all things are new- I am a new Rob.

I always like to end my story by telling about one of the great gifts God gave me. Ten years ago, on New Year's Eve, I married a wonderful Christian girl. She is what I dreamed of but I never really believed it would be possible for me to have such a wonderful wife. But God!! He gave me the desires of my heart, and now Terry and I are serving Jesus together and having the time of our lives. God is so good. And He wants to do the same thing in your life that He did for me, and that is "turn the tragedies and misfortunes of your life into something beautiful".

Rob Kesson and his wife Terry serve actively in the church. They currently are part of the core team for the Coastal Strathcona Campus, host and lead a life group, and facilitate small recovery groups through the "Freedom Sessions" course.

Rob & Terry Kesson

Chapter 3

God Is in the City

From a human perspective, it is easy to come into a city and perceive that it is void of the presence of God; yet, God is in the city and already at work before we arrive. The letter that Jeremiah writes to the Jews taken captive to Babylon by King Nebuchadnezzar, gives some key insights into how believers are to respond to God and the city in which they live. This letter is found in Jeremiah chapter twenty-nine.

Firstly, it is important to understand it is God who has placed his people in the city, regardless of the circumstances that brought them there. The Jews that were taken into captivity would have had every right to grumble about the Babylonian ghetto they found themselves in, but Jeremiah has a bigger picture to proclaim to them. In verse four he writes, "Thus says the Lord of hosts, the God of Israel, to all who were carried away captive, whom I have caused to be carried away from Jerusalem to Babylon" (Jer 29:4). Robert Linthicum in his book, *City of God, City of Satan*, explains Jeremiah is suggesting to the captives, "You are not in Babylon simply because of the exigencies of war or the particularly repressive policies of the Babylonian Empire aimed at emasculating a conquered nation. It is that God, in the Lord's infinite wisdom, needs you in the city. God needs the presence of his people in this city – and the reason for the same will become clear later on."[29] The Lord saw them not as refugees, but as people on a mission. We Christians may see ourselves as immigrants, students, or business people, but God views us as missionaries to the city.

Secondly, the church needs to realize God expects believers to fully engage with the life of the city that they find themselves living in. God did not want the captives to lead a passive life in the enemy city, while waiting for justice to be served. Instead God challenges them in verses five to seven, "Build houses and dwell in them; plant gardens and eat their fruit. Take wives and beget sons and daughters; and take wives for your sons and give your daughters to husbands, so that they may bear sons and daughters – that you may be increased there, and not diminished. And seek the peace of the city where I have caused you to be carried away captive, and pray to the Lord for it; for in its peace you will have peace" (Jer 29:5-7). God was expecting these refugees to rise up, and actively work for the peace and prosperity of Babylon. This challenge would mean that they would need to build houses and establish their families there. In the city that they now were forced to live in, God is asking them to contribute to the overall welfare of the community. God was telling these refugees, if they would take care of the city and help it prosper, they would prosper. As a result, this action would require them to focus away from themselves and the extreme hardship they were in, and to see the needs of others in the city.

For us to engage with Vancouver, we needed to ask questions like: "If we understood that the plight of the sixteen hundred homeless people on the street impacts our personal welfare, would we engage in their lives any differently?"[30] Or, "If we realized that the actions of city government affect our daily lives so profoundly, would we not be more intentional about getting involved in politics?[31] Like the Jewish people in Babylon, Christians are living in a world that is not their own. One day God will call every believer home to the 'Promised Land', but for now Christians need to ask themselves how they can play a part in promoting the 'shalom' of the city in which they live.

Thirdly, God encourages His saints that He is indeed in the city, and they are to pray for the new community they now live in. The Israelites were taken captive to a strange land after they saw their city and temple destroyed, yet in this city, God tells them to call upon Him and He would answer them. He was present in that city before they arrived. We read in verses twelve and thirteen, "Then you will call upon Me and go and pray to Me, and I will listen to you. And you will seek Me and find Me, when you search for Me with all your heart." The Jews would have been thinking, "You want us to pray for the people that carried us into captivity? These people are the enemies of God! They are the ones who destroyed our beloved city, Jerusalem! How can You expect us to pray for them?"

It is easy for Christians to isolate themselves, and pray only for their church, friends and immediate family. It is another matter, however, to pray for people who despise an individual as an immigrant to the city. God does not want His people to be bitter toward the non-Christian world that may mistreat them. Rather, He wants believers to pray for people even if they do not show the respect that every human being deserves. Jesus instructs us in Matthew 5:44, "But I say to you, love your enemies, bless those who curse you, do good to those who hate you, and pray for those who spitefully use you and persecute you." If God required these captives to settle into the ghetto of a foreign city, make plans to prosper there, and to pray for their enemies, how much more so should the Christian today? The question that believers need to ask themselves is, "Am I praying and doing all I can to be engaged in bringing about God's peace and prosperity in my city?"

Psalm 122 provides a model of how to pray for the city. This chapter begins and ends with a reference to the house of the Lord. Symbolically, I see this as the church embracing the city by praying for it. The city of Jerusalem certainly has a special place in the scriptures and in God's plan; however, the principles of how God wants His people to pray for the city they live in still applies to them today.

Both the psalmist, and Jeremiah, gives instruction to firstly pray for the peace and prosperity of the city. This prayer is not just for the righteous few, but for the entire city. God is concerned about the economic well-being of the city, because the manner with which the wealth of a city is used greatly affects the spiritual climate of an urban area. If the financial resources of the city are wisely stewarded, those who are living in poverty can be liberated, social programs can be funded, and local churches can carry out their mandate. Also, as believers we need to be aware of the dark side of money. Paul told Timothy in First Timothy 6:10, "For the love of money is a root of all kinds of evil, for which some have strayed from the faith in their greediness, and pierced themselves through with many sorrows." Therefore, the church needs to diligently pray that those with finances would be guided in the flow of wealth in our city. In this Psalm, the writer also gives instruction to, "Pray for the safety within the walls" (Ps 122). Today, more than ever, our cities need prayer for safety and for those who keep the peace. It is the responsibility of the church to pray for the protection of every citizen from conflict, crime, and vandalism against property. This prayer for safety should also include praying for those who commit crimes. The intercession of the church for these caught in the cycle of crime and violence is the greatest power to bring lasting change to these individuals.

Praying for the city should also include those who live in the "palaces." The "palace" is where the influence lies. This prayer should include the home of a wealthy citizen, the boardroom of a major cooperation, the City Hall, or the courthouse. This mandate to pray for leaders, and particularly the government, is a theme that runs throughout the Bible. Paul instructs Timothy in First Timothy 2:1- 4, "Therefore I exhort first of all that supplications, prayers, intercessions, and giving of thanks be made for all men, for kings and all who are in authority, that we may lead a quiet and peaceable life in all godliness and reverence. For this is good and acceptable in the sight of God our Saviour, who desires all men to be saved and to come to the knowledge of the truth." Here Paul makes it clear that by praying for leaders, the result will be a peace in the lives of the believer. Not only do these prayers affect the lives of Christians, they also have a profound effect on others coming to faith in Christ.

Breaking Cultural Barriers

In order to build a church in a metropolitan centre it is imperative that the church reaches out to every nationality and strata of society. On any given weekend at least sixty different nationalities are represented in Coastal Church from every walk of life.

In John 4:1–43, our Lord gives the church a plan of action in tackling the walls of racism. Tired after a long journey, the disciples headed into town to pick up some lunch while Jesus asks the Samaritan woman to give him a drink. She is shocked and somewhat indignant in her response to Jesus. First, the fact that a Jew would speak to a Samaritan, with whom there existed ethnic tension, was a surprise to her. Secondly, that he addressed her as a woman in public was a clear violation of a cultural barrier. In this setting Jesus specifically wanted to give a lesson to his disciples.

The disciples arrive not long into the conversation, and they are equally shocked to see their Rabbi speaking with the Samaritan woman, who came for water in the middle of the day. The time of her arrival at the well seems to indicate that her reputation was questionable, that she was likely shunned by the rest of the women who would arrive at the well in the cool of the day. The disciples may have wondered if she was a prostitute, adding to the tension of the moment. In this setting Jesus demonstrated that Christians are to love others even if their culture, race, gender or lifestyle offends them. Jesus honored this woman by engaging her in a conversation that would lead to her discovering that he was the Christ. He demonstrated that he truly cared about her as he listened to her and spoke into her life about her relationships. His love for her and the community was further expressed when he consented to spend two more days with them.

In the metropolitan city of Vancouver most of the people have come from another part of the world, and Coastal Church must intentionally work at being one body. In order for this to happen, we need to look past the cultural differences and see the good in others. This focus, like the Lord Jesus demonstrated with the Samaritan woman, must be on listening for the hurts in the lives of others. It is this kind of love and acceptance that will bring unity into a diverse multicultural community. Because of the way Jesus expressed His love for this Samaritan woman, verse forty-one says that many others came to believe. The church today should be a model for society where this love is demonstrated amongst great diversity. When this message is lived out, it becomes a living epistle that causes others to turn to Christ.

The Intersection of the Rich and the Poor

In the account of Jesus entering Jericho in Luke 18:35–43, and which cross-references with Mark 10:46-52, we read of the Lord's compassion for a blind beggar who reaches out in faith. After Jesus heals this man who is caught in the grip of poverty, it is recorded in Luke 19:5 that He intentionally reaches out to Zacchaeus. In doing so, Jesus demonstrates several key things that are essential to the transformation of a city.

First, Jesus shows that both the poor and the rich need our attention. Those who are disadvantaged, like blind Bartimaeus, are likely to be more vocal in their approach for help (Mark 10:48; Luke 18:38). While they need the church to respond with the healing power of Christ, Christians also need to be attentive to the less vocal cries for help from the affluent broken-hearted individual, like Zacchaeus (Luke 1:9-10). The rich must be approached despite the scorn of the religious critics. Their poverty of spirit should move the church into action as much as the beggar's impoverished condition.

Secondly, Jesus inspired a poverty relief program as He travelled through Jericho. The beggar in this town would have undoubtedly benefitted from the transformed heart of the wealthy businessman who wanted to contribute to the poor. When the rich encounter the grace of our Lord Jesus Christ, His goodness causes them to consider giving back to the poor in the community. If the church will embrace every sector and cast vision for social change in the city, I believe it is possible for transformation to occur even as it did in the town of Jericho. Surely the blind beggar was one of the first to benefit from the generosity of a converted tax crook that Jesus loved.

Thirdly, when Jesus insisted that He must go to the house of Zacchaeus, He gave an important clue on reaching the affluent (Luke 19:5). The wealthy and the influential are reached when one takes time to sit down with them in their world and hear them out. It may be their home or it could be in a social club. The key is to go to their world and engage them. If this is done graciously and authentically, it will release the finances needed to help the poor of the city and bring the needed transformation.

Nehemiah Empowered by the Holy Spirit for Action

In Nehemiah 1:4, we read that Nehemiah was weeping over the condition of his city. When a leader is moved to tears over the brokenness of a city, God now has an instrument to work with. The story of Nehemiah is a classic account of the transformation of a city that had come under siege from the enemy.

Passion and prayer alone will not bring about change. When the opportunity came for Nehemiah to present his case before the king, it was clear he was prepared to add action to his faith. In a bold move he requests a lengthy leave of absence from his job, a passport with all the needed visas to travel back to his homeland, and an open account at the king's lumber store. Passion and prayer are huge, but if the city is going to change, the "big ask" must take place. The request for finances, meeting space, permits, and so on should happen, and all done with the risk of rejection.

On arriving in Jerusalem, Nehemiah surveys the damage to the city (Neh 1:11–16). He goes out at night and inspects the work that needs to be done. In doing so, he demonstrates the wisdom of conducting a survey of the city needs, prior to engaging the people in the mission at hand. Nehemiah is symbolic of the Holy Spirit at work in the city, and like Nehemiah, the Holy Spirit has been sent by the King to be our comforter and helper. He is there at work before we arrive in the city. He guides us and consoles us as we see the darkness that has left our cities in ruin. Without the empowerment of the Holy Spirit the work would overwhelm any disciple of Christ.

Nehemiah would mobilize an entire community to rebuild the wall while under threat of attack. He does not encounter opposition from Sanballat, his enemy, until he declares the vision to rebuild the walls of the city. In Nehemiah 2:19, we read that upon hearing the plans to help the city, the enemy begins to laugh and despise them for their efforts. This type of challenge is what most church planters encounter when they set out to bring restoration to a city. When the vision is declared, the enemy brings discouragement. Nehemiah wastes no time in declaring that God will prosper him and that Sanballat has no right to be there (Neh 2:20). Likewise the church today needs to stand up to Satan and declare God has given every Christian authority and the battle belongs to the Lord!

Joe & Jessica's Story

My husband, Joseph Weiss, and I, Jessica, met in August of 2004 in San Diego, California. We met at work, soon began dating and quickly realized we had a love that lasted. I started attending Rock Church with Joe and that is where I gave my life to Jesus in May of 2005. On December 30, 2006 at the young and adventurous ages of 25 and 26 we happily married.

In July of 2007, God moved us, through Joe's job, to Vancouver, British Columbia, Canada. At first we were unsure of this move, but we prayed about it and God made it clear that this was where we were to go. Many friends and family were shocked we would leave San Diego, known as "America's Finest City", but when we crossed the border into British Columbia the sign read, "Welcome to British Columbia, The Best Place on Earth"! Wow! We upgraded!

We settled into a condo just a short distance from where Joe was working, and welcomed our first child, Joslyn in October of 2007.

A year later, 2009, I was pregnant with our second child, Caleb. Of course we had great excitement about the pregnancy and started sharing the news right away. But to our surprise the pregnancy took a shocking turn.

On just a normal day after waking up from a nap with Joslyn, I noticed that I may have had a minor accident in bed. I was embarrassed at first, but Joe insisted that I go to the doctor just to make sure everything was fine. By the time I had arrived at the doctor's I had lost even more fluid and they confirmed that I was losing my amniotic fluid. At just 19 weeks my membranes had ruptured, for an unknown reason, and I had next to nothing of the baby's amniotic fluid left. The doctors informed me that even though the baby was completely healthy that would no longer be the case moving forward.

They began to paint a very bleak picture and gave us three scenarios:

1. Labour could happen within the next 24 hours but the baby isn't viable for another 5 weeks.
2. Infection could set in within the next 72 hours in which they would have to deliver the baby and again the baby would be too little to survive.
3. We could do a termination and just start over.

We understood the severity of the issue and the risks to my health so we agreed with the doctors and went ahead with scheduling the termination. However, the following week, the week the termination was scheduled for, God planned a divine intervention and sent a couple from our life group to our door at 9:30 at night urging us to attend a healing seminar that our church, Coastal Church, was conducting with Pastor Carl-Gustav (a guest speaker from Sweden) the next day. We had known of the Healing Seminar and had planned on attending but now that labour was imminent we decided to follow the doctor's orders to stay in bed so labour wouldn't start before the appointment. That night however, with our two friends, we confessed all to the Lord, cried and prayed and the following day we made the decision to step out in faith and attend the seminar. Joe and I promised each other and God that regardless of what we would hear, see or feel from the seminar we would trust in God and believe that the baby and I were healed. We even made the decision in the car on the way to the healing seminar that we would cancel the appointment for the termination.

It was an incredible night and certainly God's presence was there. However when we went to the doctor's the following Monday to share our change of plans we were devastated to see that the water had been less than it was before, the placenta was a complete previa with no hopes of moving away from the cervix (meaning if I go into labour and it passes first I would likely need a hysterectomy to save my life) and they revealed some news that they weren't going to share with us since we were planning on terminating that our son showed markers for down-syndrome. Of course we were devastated. That was a blow we were not expecting, especially after having just been to the Healing Seminar. Thankfully, Joe was strong and he was able to look the doctor in the eye and say, "We know there is nothing you can do as doctors, nothing we can do as parents, so we are believing in God for a miracle." I took a huge gulp as he said that and the doctor answered him by saying, "There is nothing that faith can do to change the fact that your water broke at 19 weeks."

We needed strength after that meeting so on our way home we called our Pastors; Pastor Dave and Pastor Cheryl from Coastal Church for their encouragement. Pastor Dave came to our home to meet with us. We shared with him all of the medical results and we shared the worries of our families. My brother had asked me why this would happen to me if I am a good person and believe in God and I had replied to him by saying, "it wasn't God who did this, it was the devil". He then said, "now you've *really* gone off the deep end."

Pastor Dave listened to everything and then explained this was a spiritual battle and that he, the Pastoral team and the church would be fighting it for us. We shared with him that Caleb only had a 15% chance of living and even if he made it into that small percentage he only had a 3% chance of being normal. Pastor Dave responded by saying, "when I'm with God, I believe I'm in that 3%."

Another big gulp on my end but we agreed to move forward in faith. One of the things Pastor Carl Gustav said to do at the Healing Seminar was to stand on verses, write them down and stand in faith on them everyday and eventually they will carry you through the storm. So everyday I would write down a verse from the Bible in my journal and stand in faith on it. I was soaking up verses on healing and faith. They were God's promises and I was claiming them all. I was saying, "Lord, you said so...so it is true" and I was leaving no other option.

On August 25, 2009 I tuned into one of Pastor Dave's sermons and recorded the title of his sermon as my verse to stand on for the day. The verse was *1 Timothy 6:12 "Fight the good fight of faith".* Later that day at 28 weeks and 5 days, my placenta began to abrupt and I began hemorrhaging. Thankfully I was in the hospital at that time and due to how quickly I was losing blood the doctors made the call to deliver Caleb by emergency C-section. Joe was able to get there in time and after being prepped by the doctors and getting his scrubs on, he dropped to his knees in front of the Emergency Delivery Room. He knew the severity of the situation, he knew he was at risk of losing one or both of us and so he called for the glory of God to come down. Within minutes Caleb was delivered. He was born at 2 pounds and 14 ounces, however, he was born without a heartbeat as a result from the severe blood loss. The doctors stopped what they were doing and 30 seconds later, his heart started beating on its own! Glory to God!

Caleb had to put up a fight in the Neonatal Intensive Care Unit (NICU). He came in as the sickest baby at that time. He had to be paralyzed for his first 2 days of life and his little bed had to vibrate so that his lungs would stay moving. We prayed over him night and day and we were joined in prayer by our life group, our church and many others. On the dry erase board next to his bed we wrote this verse, *"The child grew and became strong, he was filled with wisdom and the grace of God was upon him." Luke 2:40.*

Finally what was only 6 days but had seemed like an exhausting journey the doctors removed his breathing tube and said he was now capable of breathing on his own now and all he needed was to grow and then he could come home! Glory to God!!! I could barely hold back the tears! Caleb was then known as the "Star of the NICU"!

A couple months later (November 2009) just about a week before Caleb's actual due date we joyfully welcomed Caleb home as a healthy and normal baby! Not a mark on his health record! Praise God!

Today Caleb is a healthy, active young five-year old boy! *"I prayed for this child and the Lord granted me what I asked of Him."* *1 Samuel 1:2*

Moving forward, the doctors said that Jessica's pregnancies would be at "high-risk". But that didn't phase us. We knew that we always wanted to have 3 maybe 4 children and we had now learned where we should put our trust. Many doctors were surprised we went ahead with another pregnancy and some would even ask if I had started leaking yet. Levi was born as a healthy full-term baby and he is our "good measure, pressed down, shaken together and running over"!

Joe and Jessica, along with their children, Joslyn, Caleb and Levi have been part of Coastal Church since 2007. They enjoy being part of Life Groups and church. Joe Weiss is the Director of Engineering at the Hyatt Regency Vancouver Hotel.

Weiss Family
(Left to right:
Jessica, Caleb, Joe,
Levi and Josyln)

1993 - Group of WHSOM students praying on the steps of King George Secondary School for Vancouver.

1994 - Coastal Church start-up phone campaign at Victory Christian Centre.

1994 - Dave Koop with the first Coastal Church Life Group in the West End.

1994 - Cheryl Koop (far right) leading worship at one the first Coastal Church Friday night services.

1994 - Dave Koop working from the first Coastal "office" in the Koop home.

1994 - Home Group meeting at The Landmark Hotel on Robson Street.

1994 – Anthony Greco, guest speaker at The Landmark Hotel ballroom.

1995 - The Koop family at The Landmark Hotel.

1998 – An early attempt at marketing with a bench ad on Robson Street.

1998 - Coastal Church moves into a second office location on Pender Street.

The Landmark Hotel

2000 – An early Alpha Course in The Lord Stanley on Alberni Street.

2001 - Allan Burnett painting during the initial move-in renovations at 1160 W. Georgia St.

2001 - The first Sunday in 1160 West Georgia building - Easter Worship

2002 - Water Baptism at English Bay. A special day for this young adults Life Group as they were all baptized together.

2002- Dave Koop having some fun with the Coastal Kids mascot, "Rovercomer".

2004 - Karl Bartel, a beloved part of Coastal Church.

2003 - Allan Burnet at a leadership training dinner for the Alpha Course volunteers.

2003 - Cheryl Koop and Clarence, our WW II vet.

2004 – Dave Koop with supporting Pastors; John Burns, Leon Fontaine, Peter VanBreda - Coastal 10th Anniversary

2003 – Henry & Norma Koop (Dave's parents).

2003 - Erwin and Dorothy Dyck (Cheryl's parents).

2004 - Coastal Church 10th Anniversary celebration service.

2005 – David and Sandra Tai handing out door prizes at the Together We Can Christmas banquet.

2004 - Police Appreciation Sunday.

2005 - Dave Koop - The "Together We Can" Campaign fund-raising banquet.

2005 – John Nixon overseeing the building renovation.

2006 - Dave Koop preaching on a Sunday morning at "Church in the Park" (Stanley Park).

2006 - One of three Sunday morning services temporarily held at The Terasen Gas Building.

2006 - Coastal Church leaders taking a tour through
2006 - Brian Taylor greeting at The Terasen Gas Building. 1160 W. Georgia St. building during renovations.

2006- A joyful baptism! (English Bay)

2006 - Easter Sunday morning - Coastal Church's first service back at 1160 West Georgia St. post renovations.

2007- Our first Christmas Eve candlelight service.

2008 - Coastal Church shoots it's first set of TV commercials (using church talent from start - finish).

2008 - Dave Koop with Ray Bakke - Chancellor of Ray Bakke Graduate University

2009 - Coastal Church hosts the first official Christian music showcase for JunoFest (Vancouver) nominated Christian artists.

2010 - A packed house for the 2010 Olympics Canadian Men's Gold Medal hockey game .

2010 - James Fam training local pastors in Haiti for Alpha GAT (Global Alpha Training).

2010 - Pastors Dave & Cheryl Koop dedicating their oldest grandson to the Lord.

2010 - Parent & Child Dedication service.

2011 - First joined Good Friday service with First Baptist Church.

2012 - Praise & Worship at the first service at the Pitt Meadows campus (Ciniplex Theatre).

2009 - Dave & Cheryl Koop meet with Bill Strickland regarding VANCAT.

2013 - Guests enjoying lunch at the monthly Business by the Book meeting.

2013 - Dave Koop & Darryl Johnson (First Baptist) serving at the joined Good Friday service (The Queen Elizabeth Theatre).

2013 - Easter Sunday morning Grand Service at The Orpheum Theatre.

2013 - Dave Koop with Prime Minister Stephen Harper - Pastors Council Meeting.

2013 - Namibia Global Alpha Training team.

2013 - Dave Koop sharing at Rogers Arena for Voices Together on Canada Day.

2014 – Easter Sunday morning, the first service at the Strathcona Campus.

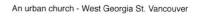

Hallelujah Point at Stanley Park

An urban church - West Georgia St. Vancouver

Fari & Angie Ghaem-Maghami.

Jen Neuman

Karen Wong

Rob & Terry Kesson

Weiss Family (Left to right: Jessica, Caleb, Joe, Levi
and Josyln)

Chapter 4

Prayer–The Work Behind the Scenes

It Starts in the Home

When we pioneered and planted Coastal Church, we naturally referred to the models of evangelism that we had seen in other churches. These models typically involved sharing our faith in Christ with those we had little or no relationship with. An example of this is what is called "street witnessing." In this form of evangelism, we went out to a busy street and handed out tracts in the hope that someone would read it and come to faith in Christ. When these models did not produce results, our team began to put their energy and time towards being with people in their homes. If their homes were too small we would meet at the local coffee shop.

On one occasion we went to the home of a couple to celebrate the birth of their son. In some communities this type of a visit would not have been a surprise, but in the spiritually barren urban landscape we were in, this visitation was unusual. We ate Filipino food that day, laughed with them, and prayed for the baby's future. That new couple became faithful members, and many of those in their circle of influence later joined our church. Today they are still in the church. The key to seeing this family and their friends embrace our church was spending time in their home building a relationship. Trusting relationships like this take time to slowly build, but once a confidence is established, they attend the church faithfully and invite others to join them. It was this approach to evangelism that resulted in people coming to faith in Christ and becoming planted in the church.

The theology for this type of approach is found in Luke 10:1-12. Here Jesus sends the seventy out on a mission trip with some clear instructions on how to reach the cities they would enter. The plan given to them is the opposite of what is often seen in churches today. The typical approach is to expect the city to come to the church, after some slick advertising or running the latest campaign. Once the "crowd" arrives, someone preaches a message about the Kingdom of God; then there is a follow up with prayer for those who were sick or needy. Finally in this approach, the church worker might sit down and have a meal in the home they are ministering to.

In Luke's Gospel, Jesus lays out a plan that reverses the order. The first thing Jesus instructs His disciples to do is to go to the homes of the people (Luke 10:5-7). The objective is to bring peace, not to see how quickly they would say the 'sinner's prayer' or accept a piece of literature. He asked His disciples to remain in the same house–in other words, get to know these people. He did not instruct His disciples to just blaze down the street, knock on a few doors, and say they had reached the city for Jesus. The church is instructed to live with the people, get in their world and then discover where they hurt and bring peace to this situation. It may be a physical illness, a rebellious child, a broken marriage, or a failing business. The point is to connect with the people in the community and their needs. Being invited into the home of a condo dweller can feel like a huge victory.

Secondly, once the church worker has come to know them well enough, the condo dweller will likely ask them to join them over a cup of tea or a meal. This is a chance to enter into their culture and see their world as they relax around food. Trust is earned slowly in the densely populated parts of our city. Once the trust is there, they will share needs and hurts they have.

Thirdly, the Lord told the disciples to heal the sick in the home (Luke 10:9). There was no invitation given to a rally at the local gathering place, but rather simple instructions to get to know the people in their homes. The power of God would be present to heal and meet the needs of humanity through the followers of Christ in the home. In Luke 10:13 Jesus cries out, "Woe to you Chorazin! Woe to you Bethsaida! For if the mighty works which were done in you had been done in Tyre and Sidon, they would have repented a great while ago, sitting in sackcloth and ashes." These works would take place in the homes of ordinary people by simple followers of Christ who cared enough to find out the hurts that were in that home. Finally, Jesus instructs the disciples in verse nine to tell them about the Kingdom of God after the relationship has been built and the felt needs of the home have been ministered to. Jesus never told us to bring the city to the church, but rather to take the church to the homes of the city.

This passage became a key for our church as we sought to find a way to overcome the challenges of building relationships with the isolated high-rise city dweller. This opposition from Satan should come as no surprise to us, as he aims to keep people tormented in darkness. As Ralph W. Neighbour writes in his book *Where Do We Go From Here?*: "The more societies he can infest with isolation, the greater are his chances of losing people to the power of Christ. His isolation has made it extremely difficult to gain access to those who need salvation."[32] However, as relationships are built with an authentic and caring love, relationships can be built leading people to Christ.

Prayer – The Key to Pioneering a Harvest

We recognized prayer to be the most essential strategy in pioneering a lasting work. For years, an enemy stronghold has existed in the heart of the city. Looking back, it is easy to see the

Lord's design in allowing me to grow up in rural southern Alberta, Canada. Here my grandfather carved a life out of the prairie soil. We grew up hearing the stories of drought, hail, prairie fires, and a land that often took them by surprise. By the time I was born, we still faced the same challenges, but the trail had been blazed, and systems were in place to contend with the attacks. As a boy I soon learned that it was all about the harvest. If we broke a new piece of land, it was done with a continual reminder that someday from this piece of sod would come a harvest. The summers were spent monitoring the upcoming harvest. Bins and combines were in readiness for when the grain was ready to be brought in. No expense was spared, and no union would have allowed the hours we worked, not relaxing until the harvest was safely in the bins. Once the harvest was in, we celebrated. It was all about the harvest.

Jesus talked about another kind of harvest. It was the great harvest of souls and their incredible value to the Father. The densely populated high-rise communities truly are great harvest fields. It is as the prophet Joel wrote in Joel 3:14a, "Thousands upon thousands are waiting in the valley of decision." And like the pioneers, Christians have been given incredible tools to take the unbroken territory and see it produce a wonderful harvest of changed lives. No tool is more important to the church pioneer than that of prayer. R.A. Torrey wrote in his book, *The Power of Prayer* that, "Prayer is the key that unlocks all the storehouses of God's infinite grace and power. All that God is, and all that God has, is at the disposal of prayer."[33] There is no frontier, no circumstance, and no restriction in any location that cannot be penetrated with the power of prayer. Prayer is as big as God, for He is behind it and stands ready to see His church built, against which the gates of hell cannot prevail. In *Circle of Prayer* Ralph Herring states that: "Prayer is God's triumph of spiritual engineering, employing all His gifts and providing unlimited access to all the resources of His being. Prayer is a summit meeting in the very throne room of the universe. There is no higher level."[34]

Pioneers are driven with a vision of the harvest. They have the faith to look past the unbroken land and the years of toil to see land producing a bountiful crop. If the love for the harvest does not drive us, we should consider our motives. The only way we can see this harvest is by lifting up our eyes. In John 4:35, the disciples could not see the harvest until Jesus pointed it out to them, and so it is with the church pioneer that we cannot see the harvest until Jesus opens our eyes to it. If we look down, we only see ourselves. If we look up, we see the needs of others. To see the harvest means we will need to not focus on ourselves, but rather look beyond our cultural barriers to see people who are ready to hear the Gospel explained in a manner they understand. This understanding will happen as we earnestly pray for those who do not know Christ. Leonard Ravenhill in his book *Revival Praying* writes, "Prayer does not condition God; prayer conditions us. Prayer does not win God to our view; it reveals God's view to us." [35] Only a God-breathed vision of humanity that is eternally damned without a personal encounter with the Lord Jesus Christ will give the pioneer the strength to pull through the long winter months. If God had not supernaturally opened the eyes of my wife and I to the great harvest of this urban centre, we would have never pointed the Gospel plow in this direction.

The pioneer understands that the first thing he or she must do is to clear the land. Stumps must be pulled and stones must be removed. This work is hard, but underneath there is the rich black soil ready to produce the harvest. Perhaps the most valuable tool the pioneer has is the plow.

Prayer is a plow. The pioneer understands that the demonic strongholds must be uprooted and the cold stones of unbelief removed. Before the blade of prayer cuts through the spiritual realm there must be a conviction by the pioneer to take hold of the plow and not let go. In Luke 9:62 Jesus says: "But Jesus told him, "Anyone who puts a hand to the plow and then looks back is not fit for the Kingdom of God" (NLT). He makes this statement to point out the cost of discipleship after someone had made the claim that he would go wherever Jesus went in Luke 9:57-60. I believe that Jesus is in the harvest field today, not wishing that any should perish. He is still beckoning us by saying, "Follow Me" as it is written in Luke 9:59. In this passage, all those who wanted to follow felt they had something to do first before accepting the call. The pioneer can have no "me first" attitude. It requires the same commitment of those who in the past conquered unknown frontiers, who burned the bridges behind them, and who pioneered the land for the next generation.

Like the plow that breaks the sod, prayer has several parallels. First, it prepares the ground for the word of God, the living seed, to be planted. As Jesus pointed out in the Parable of the Sower in Mark 4:1-9, if the seed lands on ground that is not tilled, Satan can easily come and take the seed. A study of the life of our Savior shows that after His time on the mountain in prayer that He would go down below to the multitudes, who were hungry for His word. The believer is not above His or Her Master. If Jesus needed to spend time in prayer before scattering the seed how much more should the Christian today. Prayer also brings stones of unbelief hidden beneath the ground to the surface so they can be removed.

Secondly, prayer cuts through the roots of the spiritual strongholds that have been in the area for years. As Paul explained to the church in Corinth, the weapons of our warfare are not carnal, but mighty through God to the pulling down of strongholds (1 Cor 10:4). The pioneer must be ready to persist in prayer, and be ready to feel the strain on the plow as he prays through, taking authority over the demonic strongholds in the area. Only then will those seeds that are planted have a chance to make it past the germination stage and produce disciples for Christ.

Thirdly, prayer aerates the soil, and mixes in the nutrients and fertilizer. Prayer is what gives unction to the word the pioneer preaches. Leonard Ravenhill notes in his tremendous book *Why Revival Tarries* that, "The Word does not live unless the unction is upon the preacher. Unction cannot be learned, only earned – by prayer."[36]

How each pioneer approaches his prayer strategy may vary, but the following are key essentials to consider.

The Leader Must Be a Person of Prayer

No individual is greater than his or her prayer life. As the pastors pray, so will the people pray. In this day of information overload, it is easy to be sidetracked with surveys, the latest technology, and the push to have a presentation that is contextualized for our generation. As we read in Psalm 127:1, "Unless the Lord builds the house, they labour in vain who build it." The church must realize we have something that the world cannot find, the manifested presence of God, which only comes through time spent in the prayer closet. How much pioneer work has been done in vain because the prayer closet was ignored? For the pioneer to plant a new work, it goes without saying that a vibrant prayer life is essential.

One morning I was directed by the Holy Spirit to note a key area of our downtown location. The Lord led me to Stanley Park where He first pointed out the totem pole collection. I noted they faced directly over the downtown area where we were planting the church. They represented the spiritual darkness of another god. A little further on was a memorial called "Hallelujah Point," set up to commemorate the Salvation Army, who used to gather there to sing. It too pointed across the water to the heart of the city. The next piece that also pointed over the inner city was the Nine O'clock Gun, which is still heard every evening at nine. It was at this point the Lord revealed in my spirit that there is war in the spiritual realm taking place over the heart of the city. As I stood at Hallelujah Point, the Holy Spirit spoke in my heart that we would fight this battle at the location to which it pointed. I remember thinking, "But God, the Landmark Hotel (where Coastal Church was holding services) is over to the right." Yet, today, if a person stands at this spot he will find that it points directly to where Coastal Church is located on 1160 West Georgia Street.

There have been demonic strongholds here in the past, but there are also the prayers of the saints from years ago. The battle is for the thousands that live in this high-rise community without a relationship with God. A little further past the Nine O'clock gun, there is an original surveyor's point that was used to map out city elevations. The message was clear: in order to win this battle in the spiritual realm, we need to build His church on the timeless truth in the word of God. Satan cannot resist the spoken living word that still acts like a plumb line to bring truth to a hurting world. Vancouver is a beautiful city to behold, but God was showing me what it really looked like in the spirit realm and the land that would have to be cleared before any evangelistic plan was going to work. As Peter Wagner writes in his book, *Warfare Prayer*, "... social and evangelistic programs will never work as well as they could or should by themselves if Satan's strongholds are not torn down. This is the real battle, and our weapon is prayer—warfare prayer."[37]

Develop a Corporate Prayer Life in the Church Body

Despite the fact that the life of pioneers can be very lonely, they still need the support of a community, thus the church planter needs to initiate a corporate prayer life in the early stages of the church in order to survive. The corporate prayer is needed for the lives of the new members. There is something to be gained at a corporate prayer setting that cannot be found elsewhere. We read in Acts 2:42 – 46 of how the early church met daily in homes for corporate prayer. It is in this setting that the new believer learns how to pray. The disciples must have looked back with regret on the times they could have been in prayer with their Master, but instead they were found sleeping (Matt 26:36). In the early stages of our church planting, the corporate nights in prayer were incredible times of refreshing. It was here that as a church planter I was often personally strengthened to go on. On many occasions the gifts of the Spirit were in operation, and the fresh "manna from heaven" gave us all courage to keep going. The corporate prayer meeting also serves to help the church pioneer fight the good fight of faith. As John Maxwell writes in his book *Partners in Prayer,* "Many think pastors have few problems, and they mistakenly believe that people in full-time Christian service have special favor with God that protects them for ordinary difficulties of life."[38]

Another benefit of this prayer time is that it cements the hearts of the people together. Nothing serves better than to build the love of the body like pouring your hearts out together in prayer. When the fledging congregation comes to the understanding that the pioneer needs them to help in the prayer battle, his effectiveness will multiply. The principles of this can be seen in Leviticus 26:7-8, "You will chase your enemies, and they shall fall by the sword before you. Five of you shall chase a hundred, and a hundred of you shall put ten thousand to flight; your enemies shall fall by the sword before you."

It should be noted that running a corporate prayer meeting is the last thing the devil wants a new group of believers to be doing. It is this fervent prayer that he fears the most, and so there is typically a battle that takes place in the lives of those who attend on the day of the prayer meeting. We have found that there are seasons of prayer. If we continued in the same format over a period of time the attendance and interest dropped. For a time a particular night will work well. Then perhaps at another time an early morning session would work instead. There was a period when we had a morning telephone prayer conference call at four in the morning. It was great for a season, but then there came a time when we felt like it was no longer fresh, and the Lord led us in another direction. These seasons of prayer reflected the challenges and maturing of the church. Corporate prayer is based on a trusting relationship with the Lord and with each other. By keeping the prayer meetings organic, which is in harmony with each other and the purposes of God, the meetings are alive and not legalistic. Over the years I have found little written on conducting the corporate prayer meeting.

A great exercise in corporate prayer is the prayer walk, which according to Dan R. Crawford is praying on the scene, without making a scene. There is a unique intensity in our prayers when we see, feel, touch, and hear what we are praying for. It is intercession on location.

Utilize the Power of Corporate Fasting and Prayer

The pioneer understood making sacrifices to see the harvest come in. He or she must daily lay aside his own desires to push ahead. Fasting is the ultimate shut down of the flesh. When we stop feeding the stomach which fuels the body, every other desire diminishes as we instinctively hunger for food. In Matthew 6:5 and 16, when Jesus delivered the Sermon on the Mount, He taught the multitude by saying, "and when you pray," and "when you fast." It was *when* you pray, *when* you fast, not *if* you pray and fast. Fasting is not optional, but rather vital to the success of the church pioneer.

As we look back over our short church history, we clearly see that major breakthroughs were accomplished as the church came together to fast. There is a spiritual force that breaks through the powers of darkness when we pray and fast. Our church had grown to a point where we could no longer meet in hotel breakout rooms, so we began the familiar search for a permanent home. With a conviction to stay in the heart of the city, where land is at a premium cost and no further church zoning would be given by the city, our backs were up against the wall. So as a congregation we went to the Lord in prayer and fasting asking him to show us a plan. It was in this time of fasting that the opportunity to purchase the heritage building owned by the First Church of Christ Scientist came to us. We had requested they sell it directly to us but they put it on the market, and a Muslim developer purchased it. Through an amazing set of events, this Muslim developer agreed to lease us the building at no cost until he started construction on the site. Later we found out that he had turned down a lease rate of twenty thousand dollars per month for us. I attribute this spiritual breakthrough to the power of prayer and fasting.

Over the course of the next eighteen months, we repeatedly asked the developer if he would sell us the building. Prime land such as this rarely comes on the market, and he clearly let us know he had no plans to sell it and suggested we move out of the area. We recognized that once the building was gone, so would the grandfather clause that allowed us to have a church here with a status at City Hall tax-free. Again the leadership of the church felt our only recourse was to fast and pray. We did not have the $4.365 million to purchase, but we did have a God with a wealth of promises. By now the church was accustomed to the 21-day "Daniel fast," and they had come to see that it brought incredible results. After a series of very difficult negotiations, the developer agreed to sell under some challenging conditions. God graciously brought us both the counsel and the financial support to put together the deal. Our only real asset going into this multi-million dollar deal was the power of prayer and fasting. The end result was that a prime piece of land held by the Church of Christ Scientist for over eighty years, now under the control of a developer, was put into the hands of the Lord Jesus Christ. In order to take enemy held territory, fasting and prayer is not optional, but mandatory!

Another example of the power of pioneering a work with prayer and fasting took place when we took a week to fast and pray prior to our grand opening dedication of the church building on November 3, 2002. We communicated to the congregation the purpose of the fast, and when the building was dedicated we experienced a wonderful presence of the Lord. On the day of the dedication, we broke all our records for attendance up until that time and received great support from the community. They were thrilled to see us take on the project of giving this old church a fresh life in the community, but the following day again the miraculous came through. As we read in Ephesians 3:20a there is a power that works through us. Praying and fasting allows the power of God to flow through us, allowing God to do "exceedingly abundantly above all we ask or think."

The day after the dedication, on November 4, 2002, the City of Vancouver called and asked to meet with us. They informed us of a plan to develop the property next door to us, where a 600-foot tower was to be built. The challenge for the developer of this site was that this plan exceeded the height limit by two hundred feet. In order to get the additional height, they would have to purchase this invisible two hundred feet of real estate from a neighbouring location. The owner of this location would have to agree to never use this density on the site after selling it. Since our church was a perfect candidate, the city planners called us and asked us to sell our right to build higher on our site, and also to designate our church a heritage site. It was obvious to us, and many others involved, that God was orchestrating this transaction. After several weeks of negotiations the church was awarded $4.427 million to renovate the building and to help pay down our existing mortgage. Prayer and fasting certainly had a significant role to play in this victory.

In Scripture, examples of corporate fasting are not difficult to find. In the Old Testament, Esther calls upon her people to join her in unity seeking God's divine intervention in Esther 4:16. In Ezra 8:21-23, Ezra fasted for protection as they traveled through enemy territory with their children to bring the gold back for the temple. The people of Nineveh fasted after the preaching of Jonah and changed a city in Jonah 3:5. In the New Testament, the first thing that the Apostle Paul did was fast in Acts 9:9. In Acts 13:1-3, before sending out Barnabas and Paul on that historic first pioneer missionary journey, the body of believers first came together to minister to the Lord in prayer and fasting. Jim Cymbala mentions in his book *Fresh Power*: "These men were not sitting in a boardroom making strategic charts on a whiteboard. They were not huddled around their computers working on spreadsheets. Instead they were having a time of worship, praise, and prayer, all intensified by periods of fasting."[39] Like Paul, the vanguard church will face storms that only the power of fasting can break through as seen in Acts 27:9, 39-44. If we truly want a move of God we must want it more than food. The price we will have to pay is to be ready to crucify our flesh so that the life of Christ might shine through us. Dr. Lester Sumrall comments in his book *Secrets of Answered Prayer*: "Your body doesn't want to fast either, nor do your friends want you to fast, nor does the devil want you to fast. He knows that fasting and prayer unleash the powers of heaven."[40]

Identifying the Prayer Needs of Our Church

One of the primary ways Coastal Church tracks the trends of personal needs is through the use of response cards that are filled out weekly by guests and church members in the services. Basic, yet essential information is gathered from those cards: name, address, commitments, how they found our church, prayer requests and feedback. The various ways people find the church is reflected in figure 7 below. This is a vital statistic for us to track growth, as this is very organic and constantly changing. In the early years of the church as we met in a hotel breakout rooms we observed that few people found the church based on our location. Once we moved into our facility this percentage moved from about 1 percent to 17 percent. Another example is that in the past we spent money on advertisement in the Yellow Pages. Today, with the advent of websites, we find very few people find the church in that manner. Over the years, the number one way individuals in our city find the church has been through a friend or relative; therefore, the majority of our budget goes into providing the congregation with the tools to invite their acquaintances to church. This outreach strategy may be a well-designed invitation distributed to them at a weekend service or designing our website with this initiative in mind.

We are constantly experimenting in this area. In 2009, we recruited eighty volunteers in the church, and with the help of a local producer, shot our own television commercials. These were designed to run on our local station as well as being featured on the Internet. Unfortunately, to date we have not seen the measurable results we had hoped for. Other tools that have been incorporated into attracting people are Internet social media sites such as Facebook, Twitter and Instagram, and video streaming websites such as YouTube and Vimeo. The trends suggest there has been a shift taking place with a higher percentage of people finding out about our church through these media platforms. A 2012 statistic showed that seventy percent of Canadians make use of mobile devices such as smartphones, iPads, and, or Tablets.[41] With such trends in mind and to increase our online presence, we created and released a Coastal Church official Smartphone app in September 2013. Downloaded by iPhone, iPad, and Android users, this application pools together our weekend message and life group notes, upcoming events, audio and video podcasts. It also provides a place to submit prayer requests, and provides other resources to reach, inform, and equip users for spiritual growth.

Another item that we have researched from the information on the response cards is the prayer needs. The graph below shows that the greatest need is prayer support for school and jobs.

This information is vital in helping us prepare the sermon material, Life Group notes, and special courses that are taught. Every Sunday, a prayer team gathers to pray over each individual request. If there is further follow-up needed, it is carried out during the week. As a result of being faithful and authentic in truly carrying out responses to these needs, a culture has developed where the members freely share their prayer requests in this manner.

Figure 7. Prayer Request Needs from Response Cards

Developing a Prayer Partnership of Dedicated Intercessors

The dedicated intercessors are the ones who are committed to labour with the church in prayer. They are the trusted partners with whom he or she can share the ministry challenges with. Cindy Jacobs points out the biblical precedence for this ministry in her book *Possessing the Gates of the Enemy*. She writes, "Paul wrote to the church at Ephesus asking for personal intercession and stated that he was sending Tychicus for that very purpose that they might know his affairs." [42] There are a number of ways that the church can structure the support of intercessors, but he must have dedicated prayer partners. There is no way to measure the impact of this spiritual agreement. As John Maxwell writes in his book

Partners in Prayer: "There have been times when I've gotten ready to do a service or a conference, and I've been physically exhausted. But when my prayer partners lay hands on me, and I see them praying over the auditorium, I receive a new strength-physically, mentally, spiritually, and emotionally. I feel prepared to receive the power of God." [43]

A praying church lays a foundation of prayer for generations to come. The victory we experience in seeing a harvest come into a new church plant will only be because of our prayers and the prayers of those who went before us. Our prayers will likewise affect the next generation, and so we should pray for those who are yet to come and labour in the harvest fields. This is not about our kingdom but our Lord's Kingdom. For a church to flourish in the generations to come, we first must make a deposit of prayer for those who will take our place. Our country is filled with one-generation churches, primarily because of the short sightedness in prayer.

A praying church produces praying members. Everything produces after its own kind, and a church that prays will naturally develop members who know how to go to the throne room of God. This training in prayer may not be the first item that people look for when selecting a place to worship; however, when the storms of life blow in, they are most grateful to be in a church that has taught them how to effectively pray.

A praying church will produce a holy church. God is a Holy God. If a church spends time with Him the natural outcome is a holy people.

A praying church resists the attack of the enemy. In the prayer manual entitled *Change the World! School of Prayer* it says, "It is prayer that prepares the Church for warfare, just as prayer prepares individual Christians for satanic attacks." [44]

A praying church is a place where there are signs and wonders. The world today is as hungry today as ever for the supernatural. In the postmodern world that we live in, there has been such a great hunger to see the power of God that no polished programs and moralized gospel will be able to satisfy. In order for the pioneer to break through the frontier soil, he must pray for miracles to awaken and convict those who are lost. As Peter Wagner writes in *Acts of the Holy Spirit*, "Miracles *are* signs pointing to the power of Jesus Christ and His cross to save unbelievers."[45]

It is indeed a great time to be alive and serving Christ. The fields are ready to harvest, and the church today, like no other generation, has the tools of communication, means of travel and access to volumes of information, which contribute to such a harvest. Yet the most powerful tool to build the church has not changed: it is the power of prayer.

Karen's Story

I was born and raised in Venezuela and into a traditional Chinese family with loving and hardworking parents, who gave me and my sisters the best of everything. Though my family had no Christian background, they enrolled me and my sisters in one of the best Catholic schools in the city. This is where I learned a bit about God, and then equated Him as the One who gave us rules that were hard to follow.

Despite having it all, during my formative years, I lived life on the gloomy side, feeling sandwiched between two contrasting expectations from different cultures. I thought that my parents were not pleased with me, so I always did things to gain their love. I was always depressed. In fact, even my grandfather would always complain to my parents asking them why his granddaughter walked around with a bitter face. Such darkness grew as I believed that I was not good enough, not smart enough, and not beautiful enough. After graduating from high school in 1994, I was done with being depressed, and the decision to build my own life came. I figured that if I did more, learnt more, travel more, my life would be fulfilled. Surely then, I thought, this would stop the darkness and low self-esteem waves that kept flooding into my spirit and soul.

And hence, I became the master architect of my life. As so, I built my life by doing more for others. I did everything to please my parents and friends in return of more attention and love. I built my life by learning more so I could achieve more. I thought that if

I excelled in my studies, I would be seen as confident, capable, and it would give me identity. After pursuing years of higher education in Venezuela and then in Canada, I was left unsatisfied. I built my life by travelling around Europe gaining fleeting adventures, yet feeling so empty.

Then I pursued the idea of being in a relationship, thinking that a boyfriend would complete me. I did find one, but it ended to be an unhealthy and heartbreaking relationship. At that point I realized that whatever I built did not bring happiness, completeness, and purpose.

Yet in all these things, God was working in the background and set it up one day for me to meet a guy in a dancing event, where we became friends. After seeing the despair in my face, he invited and brought me to Coastal Church one Sunday in 2001.

I had been exposed to other churches, but Coastal was different. When I came in, my attitude was.. *"I know all about God, so why am I here?"* I had enough bad experiences of church when growing up, and I didn't believe in it. The message that day was titled "Finding the love of your Life" which really caught my attention because that's what I wanted to do. At some point Pastor Dave said we could never be complete and happy with a boyfriend or a spouse, until we are complete and one with Jesus. I was speechless.

With tears in my eyes I kept thinking of my empty life and darkness in my heart. I desperately needed Jesus to complete me. So, when Pastor Dave gave the invitation to receive Jesus' forgiveness and love, I sincerely prayed, and reached out to Him. I did not understand everything then, but I knew I needed to make that decision.

Now Jesus was part of my life. I was attending church services, and started to learn who Jesus really was through the Alpha Course. Quickly after this I started to date that friend who brought me to church. I thought, *"hey, this is pretty good. I have a boyfriend and I have Jesus!"*

Slowly The Holy Spirit brought me to the realization that I had not placed Jesus as number one. Instead of worshiping Him,

I worshiped my boyfriend who became *everything* to me. This led to an unhealthy relationship which ended the year after. I was devastated. It was as if a hurricane had stormed through my building and torn it to pieces. My life was not built on strong foundation, but on sand.

The following year, I made a heartfelt commitment to let Jesus be the Chief Architect and let Him re-build my life completely. Jesus helped me put down the old structures in my life–that is anything I had built for selfish purpose. He graced me to release my painful experiences, and senseless plans, and that's when I felt compelled to draw nearer to Jesus, who was really my only hope.

The next process was intense. Jesus removed the weak foundation through Celebrate Recovery, a program we had then at Coastal Church. He revealed that I was basing my self-image on what others would say of me, instead of what God says about me, and I needed to change that old thinking. I admitted I was co-dependant. I was also bitter because I thought I wasn't loved by others, and felt like a failure as a result. It was painful to go through this. However, by His Grace, I asked God for forgiveness for my attitude, and eventually I was able to forgive myself and others.

Then it was time for Jesus to put a proper foundation in me. God continued the good work and put a desire in me to know Him more. I then understood that His love for me is not based on my performance and achievements. He loves me because I am valuable to him. He considered me so worthy that He took the punishment for my worst actions and attitudes, so I could have an abundant life here on earth, and an everlasting life with Him. I didn't need to strive to gain love by others or God Himself. Jesus set me free from fearing or pleasing people.

This foundation process continued in 2004 and 2005, where Jesus led me to take the Master's Commission program, a full-time internship, under the mentorship of Pastors Dave and Cheryl, and Donaleisa Leavers. It was construction time, building according to God's way and that entailed hard work!

During this internship, I learned to put God's word in my heart so I would not fall back into my old ways of thinking and behaving. I had the opportunity to learn how to pray and talk to God on a daily basis, and the joy to recognize His voice.

It was during this foundational period that I got to "do more", "learn more", and "travel more" with a godly purpose. Now my heart was healthier, complete with Jesus, which enabled me to serve in the church out of the fullness of my heart.

Today, Jesus is still rebuilding my life. He lifted me up from the ground, reconstructed my life for the better. I am still a work in progress. Jesus is constantly working in me, and building me up. God gave me purpose. He has shown me that He didn't create me by accident. He placed me in a Chinese family in a Latin country, and then moved me to Canada for a purpose. It was all in His plans that I would be able to relate to different cultures, and do His work. All the experiences I went through have allowed me to serve our current Coastal interns to help them grow strong in Christ.

If you were to ask me how tall my building is now, I would say not very tall. But it is at the level that I can serve through missions, serve interns and apprentices, and now humbly serve as an associate pastor here at my home church, Coastal Church. Never did I think I would be doing what I do today.

Karen Wong

Without Jesus, my life would be still a shack. With Him my life is redeemed, and revitalized for His purpose. It is a privilege to be part of the plan to build His church, and be His hand to see others being equipped, empowered and built up in Him.

Karen Wong serves as an assistant pastor at Coastal Church and oversees the Biblical Studies department, internship and apprenticeship program. She loves serving in many other areas in God's house.

Chapter 5

Serving the City

In order to function as a healthy church we must understand and practice servanthood truths. The key to being a great church in any city is to serve its community. As Jesus said in Matthew 20:25- 26, "You know that in this world kings are tyrants, and officials lord it over the people beneath them. But among you it should be quite different. Whoever wants to be a leader among you must be your servant."

The world measures success by the number of people who serve you, God measures success by the number of people you serve. The only way you can serve God is by serving the people in your city. You cannot serve God directly. It is in serving others that you serve God, and God wants us to do it in community, in relationship to others.

To be a servant is all about attitude: a mind set, a mental view, a frame of mind (how you frame your world in your mind). This servant attitude does not come naturally to us but requires training.

Training for Service

The introductory leadership training for the church consists of membership classes called The Connect Course and the Alpha Course. The Connect Course consists of the following classes: a history of the church and the core values; a study on the essential habits of a believer; a teaching and survey that reveals an individual's spiritual gifting; and an overview of missions in the local church; and training on how to lead a small group. The Alpha Course serves as a new believer's class, providing training on the basics of Christianity. Once a member has completed the introductory training, there are a number of different options available. These options include advanced Bible courses, marriage training, financial seminars, and other specialized courses.

Most people would rather "do" church than simply be a spectator. So on any given weekend there are hundreds of volunteers that are helping at the weekend services. The Connect Course enables us to see the talents and gifting that each person has. When we discover that as individuals we are gifted with different abilities, it helps us understand the unique qualities in others in the church. Serving at church is not only a great opportunity to give, but also a chance to connect and build great friendships. Over the years we have seen that by volunteering in the church people have become more aware of their purpose and why they were created with a certain qualities.

We believe in the God-given potential of the next generation, and with our church growth, we increased our leadership training by re-tooling a full-time discipleship program named Master's Commission which ran in 2003-2005. In 2011, the Coastal Internship program was put in place and designed to provide a platform for emerging young leaders to establish a strong spiritual foundation, obtain hands-on ministry opportunities, with the aim to developing them as servant leaders within our church. As of 2014 we have seen thirty nine young individuals equipped for life through the program since the inaugural year, and at least eighteen of them have assumed various leadership roles, such as Life group leaders, Children's Church teachers, Young Adult ministry, etc. Another level of ministry training has been included in 2014 through a one-year apprenticeship, giving opportunity to young leaders desiring to be trained to fulfill a ministry call within the church.

Our approach as a church is to equip every member with the fundamentals of Christianity and the training to serve in some area of the church. At any given time, approximately 30 percent of the congregation are people who will only attend the church for a year or less. In a sense, the church is like an airport, where people are landing and taking off on a regular basis. As people come to faith in Christ during their time staying in Vancouver, they develop a vision to make disciples in their nations. Our leadership sees this training as an investment in the global church. We understand that some of them will move on shortly after they are equipped to serve in a particular area; however, this short season of being welcomed to join the team has an amazing reach around the world. When the time comes for them to move, they are ready and willing to serve in the next city they live in. For those who remain in Vancouver, or have always lived here, our goal is to see them equipped and actively serving.

We have seen this in the case of many young Australians who come to work on the local ski slopes for the winter. During their time here they received an invitation to church. Since church provides another way to explore the culture of the city and possibly satisfy their spiritual curiosity, they investigated one of the services and the Alpha course. In the months that follow they encountered Christ and end up attending a small group. Today in Australia there are a number of small groups being led by them and other people who only had a short stay in urban Vancouver. The training they received here in a few months was enough to send them back as missionaries to their own land.

Another example is that of a young Persian woman who attended the church over the summer months. She accepted

Jesus Christ as her Lord in one of the small groups that was conducted in the Farsi language. In the short time she was here, she was invited to the various training programs we had available and was given a chance to serve. Prior to her returning to her home city of Dubai, she was water baptized in the Pacific Ocean only a few blocks from the church. Today she leads a small group in her city and baptizes converts in the pool located in her home despite the threat of imprisonment.

Serving with Others

The 2010 Winter Olympics proved to be a wonderful example of how churches can come together to serve. "More Than Gold," which is comprised of a network of denominations, churches, Christian institutions, and individuals, had been asked by the Vancouver Organizing Committee to assist them throughout the 2010 Winter Olympics and Paralympics with hospitality. It was a privilege for Coastal Church to be involved with this movement from the early stages. The results are a clear example of what can take place as churches collaborate together.

During the Olympics, our church was able to serve in a number of different ways. One way was to dispense over fifty thousand cups of complimentary hot chocolate or coffee to thousands as they entered the Translink stations, our transit system. In addition to that, the volunteers served over two hundred cups of hot coffee to the residents on their way to work. Approximately eight hundred volunteers from the church stepped up to make these services happen. The Vancouver Police Department wrote up in their reports the amazing calming effect our efforts had on the city, and on the crowds waiting in line to get on the trains. This type of radical volunteering not only has a deep impact on the community, but also has a deep impact on those serving. I have observed that when God is at work, the people hunger to be involved. David talks of this in Psalm 110:3, "Your people shall be volunteers in the day of Your power."

As the Olympic torch was paraded past the church building the morning of the opening ceremonies, we served fifteen hundred pancakes to the community for this historical event. At numerous concerts, hockey games, and hundreds of pieces of literature were given out during the course of the games. This outreach would not have happened if our church had attempted to do this in a solo fashion. By joining hands with the Salvation Army, volunteers from YWAM, Southern Baptists from Texas, and other partners of "More Than Gold," we were able to make a tremendous impact on our community and the world.

During the Olympics, one of our goals was to communicate to our neighbours that the church was an open and inviting place. These residents who live next to us walk by the church on a daily basis, but many of them never notice the church. By serving our community, as described above, we were praying that their interest would be piqued. Fred and his wife fit that description. They live only two blocks away, and by Fred's own admission, he is not sure if he is an atheist or a seeker who is ready to investigate Christianity; however, Fred loves hockey, and when he found out that the games were shown live in high definition on the big screen at the church, he came. Over a hamburger and a coke he explained he did not know churches could be as open as this.

Fred, like so many others, was hungry for a place to belong in the city. As he looked around he acknowledged the openness he was enjoying came from our faith. This hospitality was enough of a reason for him to come and check out the Sunday services. As the Games continued, a very encouraging thread emerged from the comments we received. People were noticing a change on our block. Radical hospitality was connecting people in an otherwise cold concrete jungle. One of the keys to having them embrace the hospitality was seeing a church work alongside other familiar organizations like the Salvation Army.

Another goal was that Coastal Church hoped to send a message to the nation that the church as a whole is inviting them to be part of the dialogue on spiritual matters. In a surprising way we had an opportunity to do this. For Canadians, the most defining moment of the 2010 Winter Olympics was winning the men's gold medal in hockey during overtime. This game took place during the time slot of our third service on Sunday. Rather than resist the timing of it, we announced to the church it was "Jersey Sunday," and invited them to bring their friends and cheer on the game in the sanctuary. National media picked up on this idea, and a television crew came to announce to Canadians that the church was joining the rest of Canada in cheering. With the stained glass windows in the background, close to six hundred fans waved and shouted as Canada scored the overtime goal. The broadcast featured the church for only a few moments, but I hope a message was sent that the church is ready to engage in a conversation or discussion with them.

The Olympic Games provided a chance to build relationships with other Christian organizations, like we had not seen before. Like any relationship, it took an investment of time and money. It also meant working through misunderstandings, but in the end, we know that we played a role in bringing measurable changes to the heart of the city.

In 2009, a new initiative to bring churches together emerged as a result of heartfelt prayer and collaborative meetings with local leaders from major denominations. Having been part of such discussions, I believe these key relationships are strengthened, bringing a greater church unity with the vision to exalt God in Vancouver. Out of this cross-pollination, the goal was to see fresh initiatives with lasting results.

One such initiative was to hold a joint service of the leading churches. We were excited to see this come to pass as we held a joint Good Friday Service on Friday, April 8th, 2011 with First Baptist Church. This joint service was a first in my twenty years of pastoring here and was a historical moment of transformation for Vancouver. Since then, we have held yearly joint Good Friday services where First Baptist and Coastal Church have worshipped together.

On July 1st, 2013, Coastal Church took part in a monumental event called Voices Together. This event gathered the Christian community of Vancouver, and the Lower Mainland, on Canada Day for a time of unified prayer and worship at Rogers Arena. As a church we were privileged to be part of the core planning team along with other interdenominational ministries and local church leaders. Personally, this stretched my leadership as I saw the timing of this project coincide with a growing role to provide spiritual leadership in the city.

To meet with other leaders and pray with them takes effort. It requires leaders to clear their schedule and focus on the bigger picture. Leaders cannot wait for another individual to come over with a welcoming gift and ask if they would like to join in prayer. In coming together to pray, it is important to find common ground and sincerely pray for others in a way that is sensitive to their background. Satan is hard at work to breed suspicion and encourage independence. This attitude drives us to pride, isolation, and division. On the other hand, we can be sure the Holy Spirit will be nudging us to a life of unity even as Jesus prayed that we would be one. In order to reach the harvest, the Lord will require that leaders labour in prayer with diverse church leaders. God in His infinite wisdom created this incredible diversity. Even as He created no two snowflakes the same, He also birthed many wonderful diverse congregations. Just as there are many different flavours of ice cream, there are many different flavours of churches. It is essential however that people see that we are on the same side. It has been our experience that the unchurched community is attracted to a church that does not have the attitude that they are the only ones with the answer. When they see that the church has a relationship with other churches, it gives them a sense of security that lessens their hesitation to cross the threshold of the church.

Serving in the Marketplace

Since the church is uniquely located in a combined commercial and residential zone in the city, we currently have a monthly outreach event to the marketplace. Every first Wednesday of the month the church hosts an outreach luncheon event called "Business by the Book." Our approach here is somewhat different than other ministries that operate in the downtown core, in that our goal is not just to reach the "corner office" crowd. The luncheon takes place in an office tower across the street from our church building and attendance averages over one hundred. At this luncheon, various business leaders share their testimonies of how they came to faith in Christ and key principles of leadership. In this setting, we encourage young leaders to take active roles in organizing and running the event. By promoting their profession as a calling and granting them an opportunity to serve Christ with it, we have seen them flourish and be inspired to invite colleagues to church.

Our mission's strategy includes taking businessmen and women to other countries to grant them an opportunity to pass on their skills in underdeveloped countries. One example is a team that went to Mongolia in 2008. Here, we partnered with Asian Outreach and the local university and taught a three-day marketing seminar. This trip resulted in our team utilizing their skills, sharing their faith in Christ, and a cross-pollination of business ideas.

Serving with the Community

The city is effectively changed when leaders join together to serve. It has been my experience that when those within various organizations reach out and try to work with other groups, there are seldom any lasting results; however, when the leaders of these groups come together and agree, lasting changes can be made. These decision makers are the ones who hold the influence and control the budgets.

In 2010, I met with Major Susan Van Duinen, Division Commander for the Salvation Army in British Columbia, where she expressed that what was lacking was an inventory of current and ongoing initiatives in the city. Too often churches or organizations spend valuable capital in launching a new endeavor without realizing this same work is already underway in the city. If stronger communication lines existed between leaders, new endeavors could be better planned with a spirit of cooperation among organizations. For instance, there was a situation that arose where it was communicated to the Salvation Army that a new recovery centre was being planned in the neighbourhood where they currently operated one. When the Salvation Army heard about this they withdrew their service and invested their time and resources in another area of the city.

As a local church in a densely populated area of the city with space at a high premium, we intentionally have formed alliances with groups offering services we cannot. It is important to establish what a church's calling in the city is and to do that well. For example, on a regular basis people come to our facility looking for groceries, but we lack the space for a food bank; however, we support the Vancouver Food Bank, both financially and by offering volunteers, and in doing so we can direct those outside the church family to the Food Bank for help, thus producing a win-win solution for both organizations.

Working with those who need drug and alcohol rehabilitation is another example of this. In 1996 I met with Maurice McElrea, president of Union Gospel Mission. He passionately asked us not to start a centre in the city to treat those battling addictions. Since 1940 they have worked in the city helping the homeless and those caught in this cycle. It made more sense for us to support them with prayer and financial support. Instead he challenged me to find a location to have a Coastal Church campus in the neighbourhood to welcome the graduates from their program. In 2014, 18 years after Maurice gave us this challenge, we were able to establish our Strathcona campus just a block away. Here people from all walks of life in the community come to worship.

Our "Police Appreciation Sunday", an event which took place in 2006 and 2008, has proven to be another way of honouring and serving our community. The idea started after we had a false alarm in our building late one night. The officers arrived at the building and I did a walk through with them. As we left the children's church area I looked back to see one of the officers pausing at the wall with a strange look on his face. After we wrapped up the call, my curiosity brought me back to the wall. A poster hung here with a picture of children praying for the protection of our police officers. At that time the Lord spoke to our hearts to dedicate a Sunday to praying for them and showing them public support, which they seldom receive.

I shared this idea with an ex-police officer from another church. As the owner of a security company in the city, he set up an appointment with me to meet the police inspector in our area of the city. She met with us, but was extremely skeptical. One of her concerns was that this would turn out to be a publicity stunt for our church. I explained to her that our intention was first to show public support for their work and pray for them. We also wanted to use this as an opportunity to let the youth and children see the police in a positive light. I explained to her that most people have very little idea of what a day in the life of an officer consists of. I asked her to give a fifteen minute talk on that subject. The sermon would be the other fifteen minutes based on the Good Samaritan. We left the office only with a commitment that she would review it with the police chief. A week later she called to tell us she would be glad to do it, and would bring with her the police dogs, motorbikes, and the horses used to patrol well-known Stanley Park.

On a warm sunny day in June, the traffic outside our building slowed to a crawl, as horses, dogs, motorbikes, and patrol cars were all parked outside the church. Children were sitting on the horses; teens were having their pictures taken with an officer beside his

Harley Davidson motorcycle, and even parents lined up to ask for a card similar to a baseball card for the police dogs. As the day was winding down, I told one of the motorcycle officers how much it meant for us to have them there that day. He was quick to respond and tell me I had no idea what it meant to them. He said on this particular day, they had an assignment to police a demonstration that was against the Vancouver Police Department for the way they had handled a recent incident. With tears in his eyes this officer said he was not a church attendee, but today he saw God at work. The inspector was also deeply moved as she came by to thank me. She told us that in her twenty-five years on the force, no church had ever done anything like this for them in the city.

Today we have police officers in the church as a result of these appreciation days. Several young men who sat in those services realized that God was calling them to serve as policemen and understood that the church would support them wholeheartedly. One of the senior officers, who helped arrange the event, came to church, gave his life to the Lord, and was later water baptized.

Coastal Church has also taken a lead role in the performing arts community, an example being showcasing the Gospel genre for the Juno Awards. These awards are the Canadian equivalent of the Grammy Awards in the United States. In 2009, Vancouver had the privilege of hosting the JunoFest Christian Showcase, featuring Juno Award nominee Christian artists. Numerous events were held around us. Next door, the Shangri-La Hotel was hosting celebrities and parties. A few blocks away various nightclubs opened their venues to showcase different genres of music. On the front of our building hung a banner that was sanctioned by the Juno committee, declaring our auditorium to be one of the venues for this prestigious event in the city. The effect of hosting the event in our church was interesting. The community certainly did notice and so did the media. Once again, we were breaking ground, and our willingness to steward our facility for this event caused them to be curious enough to come and ask questions. Having a venue such as this one is a privileged position. Peter

Block addresses the responsibility that comes with stewardship in his book Stewardship: Choosing Service over Self Interest. He writes, "...[o]ne intent of stewardship is to replace self-interest with service as the basis for holding power and using power[46]."

In having various Juno nominees perform at this showcase event, we also introduced up and coming artists within our congregation. This introduction provided an elevated platform for them, and sends a message to the church congregation that we believe in the artists within our church. Another benefit was that this project proved to be a catalyst for others to use their gifts. As a result of reaching out our hands to support the Gospel recording artists, gospel music will be showcased in the years to come in the cities that host the Junos. To us, this looked like urban transformation.

Chapter 6

Conclusion

A round the world today there is a migration of humanity to the city. This growth is generating communities of high-rise dwellers. In each of these urban centres God is calling leaders to contextualize the situation and establish His presence with vibrant churches. The manner in which God brought about Coastal Church was unique, but the principles that led to this model can be duplicated elsewhere. As I reflect on what has transpired at the church over the past twenty years, these are some key principles I have noted as relevant.

1. *Prayer and fasting.* Every city has demonic strongholds that need to be broken, and the power of prayer and fasting is essential to take ground. Our church leadership team found that it consistently moved the obstacles we faced. Every office and piece of land we took only came about after a season of focused corporate prayer and fasting.

2. *Persistence.* Every week in the downtown of a city, you can watch another store or business close their doors and move on. The city is calloused to the start-up and failure of new ventures. Respect from urban dwellers comes slowly, but if the church planter refuses to quit, the residents of

the high-rise community will pay attention and will begin to support the work.

3. *Build relationships on every level.* Relationships are currency for the church. Ultimately, it is the intangible product that we "sell" in the hustle and bustle of the city life. Firstly, the vertical relationship with our Heavenly Father must be cultivated privately and publicly for a lost and dying world to see. Secondly, the family relationships of the church planter must be guarded at all costs. There is always another city that needs a church, another job that can be taken, but the highest calling is to build and model a godly family and home. Thirdly, investments into the church family and neighbourhood must be made. There is not a quick return on this investment of time, and it is normal to expect three to five years before people begin to give back into the work. Fourthly, build relationships with other Christian leaders in the community. The experience of these individuals is a valuable resource; moreover, the mutual strength that is established by these relationships is essential for staying committed to the cause. Fifthly, by reaching out to the leaders in the marketplace and the political arena, an alliance can be built that will serve to help the church planter gain a visible foothold.

4. *Learn the language of the tribe.* The high-rise community is one of the most unreached mission fields of the world today. Each tower is essentially a guarded tribe that has a culture and language the church worker needs to learn. This requires an incarnational approach, as it is the subtle little things that open up the communication so the gospel can be presented.

5. *Consistency.* Throughout our twenty years, the Coastal Church leadership found it to be extremely beneficial to stay in one location. For the first seven years we met in the same hotel and fought to keep a consistent location. By providing a consistent location, culture and identity in the

church, a sense of safety is portrayed that attracts the urban dweller. This is essential in giving confidence to existing members in inviting their friends and relatives to church.

6. *Study other models in the world.* Some of the ideas we found to work came from visiting other churches in the world with similar challenges. For example, in Singapore Cheryl and I visited New Creation Church that ran multiple Sunday services, and the children met in different buildings in the downtown area. We explored their model and incorporated many of the innovations of this church into our structure. Another example was learned from Pastor Mitri Raheb and his leadership team at the Evangelical Lutheran Christmas Church in Bethlehem. This church has developed an arts program that has brought healing for the youth of the city, which has resulted in a tangible lasting transformation. As a result of this inspiring model, Coastal Church today is collaborating with an extensive arts program.

7. *The theology of a building.* Wherever a church meets, it silently speaks twenty four hours a day to the residents of the city. While it may not be possible to own a building, or even rent a facility exclusively seven days a week, the church planter can ensure that the location, the decoration, the cleanliness and the atmosphere reflect quality and warmth. Urban dwellers have a high expectancy for excellence, and if it is there they are much more inclined to come and listen. If all possible, a visible sign of Christianity like a cross, speaks of the presence of Christ in the city.

8. *Keep the teaching practical.* One of the common remarks that come back to the Coastal leadership team is that the teaching has been relevant and practical for everyday living. It has been our experience that urban dwellers are informed consumers, and this translates to individuals

who look for practical insight after spending time in church.

The principles listed here are nothing new, but what is new is the changing landscape of missions in the world. Our Lord Jesus Christ commanded us to go into all the world, and it is my prayer that God would raise up great pastors for the "world" found in the modern high-rise cities of the 21st century.

Lessons Learned

For the leaders of Coastal Church and the congregation, it truly has been a privilege to witness, by the grace of God, a lasting change in the spiritual climate in the downtown core of Vancouver. Principles of planting an inner city church, under the shadows of office towers and apartment buildings, were slowly etched out.

Certainly the principle of building relationships has been a thread that is essential for the fabric of this community. The vertical relationship with our Heavenly Father must be foremost for the leader and each member. Horizontal relationships within our family units, our small groups, our congregational services, our neighbouring churches, and those within the community are needed for the well being of this organic church.

Out of these relationships must persist a love for the hurting and the lost in the City of Vancouver. It is our duty to remain faithful to preach and live the never-changing Gospel of our Lord Jesus Christ. In doing so, we will continue to do our best to equip new believers to be dedicated disciples of Christ, believing that some will be genuinely called to lead the next generation.

We have come to realize that a building on the ceremonial street of the city is a powerful principle of God at work in the city. As the residents come and go there is a witness that the abundant life that Christ promised is found in the modern urban world. It has been an amazing journey, but there is much yet to learn and to be discovered in bringing a transformational impact in the high-rise community of Vancouver.

If one looks closely on 1160 West Georgia Street, Vancouver, there is at street level a ten-foot tall rustic cross that silently speaks. Jesus is still calling for all those who are weary and need rest.

Coastal Church. 1160 West Georgia Street.

Bibliography

6S Marketing, "Infographic: Canadian Internet Usage Statistics on Mobile, Search and Social" http://www.6smarketing. com/blog/infographic-canadian-internet-usage-statistics/ (Accessed July 7, 2014)

Adeney, Miriam. *Daughter of Islam: Building Bridges with Muslim Women.* Downers Grove, IL: InterVarsity Press, 2002.

Bakke, Ray. "The Challenge of World Evangelization to Mission Strategy." In *Planting and Growing Urban Churches: From Dream to Reality.* Edited by Harvie M. Conn. Grand Rapids, MI: Baker Book House Company, 1997.

___. *A Theology as Big as The City.* Downers Grove, IL: InterVarsity Press, 1997.

Bakke, R., and J. Hart. *The Urban Christian: Effective Ministry in Today's Urban World.* Downers Grove, IL: InterVarsity Press, 1987.

Barna, George. *Revolution.* Carol Streams, IL: Tyndale, 2005.

Bell, Rob. *Velvet Elvis, Repainting The Christian Faith.* Grand Rapids, MI: Zondervan, 2005.

BizMapBC. The Vancouver Economic Development Commission. "Downtown Vancouver (DVBIA) Neighbourhood Profile,

2009." http://www.bizmapbc.com/neighbourhood-profiles/downtown-neighbourhood.pdf (accessed March 30, 2010).

Block, Peter. *Stewardship: Choosing Service Over Self-Interest.* San Francisco, CA: Berrett-Koehler Publishers, 1993.

Bloom, David E., and Tarun Khanna, "The Urban Revolution," *Finance and Development. A Quarterly Magazine of the IMF* (September 2007). http://www.imf.org/external/pubs/ft/fandd/2007/09/bloom.htm (accessed March 30, 2010).

C3 Church Vancouver. "Connection." http://www.c3v.ca/connection (accessed March 30, 2010).

Campus Crusade for Christ. "The Jesus Film – Video." http://www.campuscrusade.com/Jesus_Film/2_hour_jesus_video.htm (accessed March 30, 2010).

Chandler, Maggie. "West End Real State Analysis." Vancouver Reflections. www.vancouverreflections.com/category/west-end/ (accessed March 30, 2010).

City of Vancouver – Community Services, Housing Centre. "Homelessness in Vancouver." http://vancouver.ca/commsvcs/housing/homelessness.htm (accessed March 30, 2010).

Clegg, T., and W. Bird. *Lost in America: How You and Your Church Can Impact The World Next Door.* Loveland, CO: Group Publishing, 2001.

Cole, Neil. *Organic Church Growing Faith Where Life Happens.* San Francisco, CA: Jossey-Bass, 2005.

Comiskey, Joel. *Reap The Harvest: How a Small-Group System Can Grow Your Church.* Houston, TX: Touch Publication, 1999.

Conn, Harvie. *Planting and Growing Urban Churches: From Dream to Reality.* Grand Rapids, MI: Baker Book House Company, 1997.

Cordeiro, Wayne. *Doing Church as a Team*. Ventura, CA: Regal Books, 2001.

Crawford, D. and C. Miller. *Prayer Walking*. Chattanooga, TN: AMG Publishers, 2002.

Cymbala, Jim. *Fresh Power: What Happens When God Leads and You Follow*. Grand Rapids, MI: Zondervan, 2001.

Dawn, M., and E. Peterson. *The Unnecessary Pastor: Rediscovering The Call*. Grand Rapids, MI: William B. Eerdmans Publishing Company, 2000.

Eastman, Dick. *Change the World School of Prayer*. Studio City, CA: World Literature Crusade, 1983.

Emerson, M., and C. Smith. *Divided by Faith: Evangelical Religion and the Problem of Race in America*. New York, NY: Oxford University Press, 2000.

Finney, Charles G. *Revivals of Religion*. Chicago, IL: The Moody Bible Institute, 1962.

First Baptist Church, BC. "Ministry Plan. Final Report of the 20/20 Vision Renewal Committee for 2006/07." Report presented to the Church Council of First Baptist Church, Vancouver, BC, February, 2007.

Fox, Andrew. *The Apprentice Leader: Learning to Serve as a Senior Leader*. Kent, WA: Sovereign World, 1999.

Gibbs, Eddie. *Church Next: Quantum Changes in How We Do Ministry*. Downers Grove, IL: InterVarsity Press, 2000.

Global Day of Prayer. "Global Day of Prayer – History." http://www.globaldayofprayer.com/history.html (accessed March 30, 2010).

Gospel Herald, Global Chinese Service. "Interview: More Than Gold CEO on Winter Olympics 2010 in Vancouver." *The Gospel Herald, Global Chinese Service* (February 14th, 2010) http://www.gospelherald.net/article/opinion/45054/interview-more-than-gold-ceo-on-winter-olympics-2010-in-vancouver.htm (accessed March 30, 2010).

Government of Canada. "Population by Selected Ethnic Origins by Census Metropolitan Areas (2006 Census)." Statistics Canada. http://www40.statcan.ca/l01/cst01/demo27y-eng.htm (accessed March 30, 2010).

Government of Canada. "Proportion of Foreign-born Population, by Census Metropolitan Area (1991 to 2001 Censuses)." Statistics Canada. http://www40.statcan.ca/l01/cst01/demo47a-eng.htm (accessed May 3, 2010).

Government of Canada – Statistics Canada. "NHS Focus on Geography Series- Greater Vancouver, 2011." http://www12.statcan.gc.ca/nhs-enm/2011/as-sa/fogs-spg/Pages/FOG.cfm?lang=E&level=4&GeoCode=5915020 (accessed June 25, 2014).

Grenz, Stanley J. *A Primer on Postmodernism.* Grand Rapids, MI: William B. Eerdmans Publishing Company, 1996.

Guder, Darrell L. *Missional Church: A Vision for the Sending of the Church in North America.* Grand Rapids, MI: William B. Eerdmans Publishing Company, 1998.

Hartcourt, M., and K. Cameron, with S, Rossiter. *City Making In Paradise: Nine Decisions that Saved Vancouver.* Vancouver, BC: Douglans & McIntyre, 2007.

Harvard Business Essentials. *Your Mentor and Guide to Doing Business Effectively. Coaching and Mentoring: How to Develop Top Talent and Achieve Stronger Performance.* Boston, MA: Harvard Business School Publishing Corporation, 2004.

Henderson, D. Michael. *John Wesley's Class Meeting: A Model for Making Disciples.* Nappanee, IN: Evangel Publishing, 1997.

Henderson, J., and M. Casper. *Jim & Casper Go to Church: Frank Conversation about Faith, Churches, and Well-meaning Christians.* Carol Stream, IL: Tyndale House Publishers, 2007.

Herring, Ralph. *Circle of Prayer.* Wheaton, IL: Tyndale House Publishers, 1974.

Jacobs, Cindy. *Possessing the Gates of the Enemy.* Grand Rapids, MI: Baker Publishing Group, 2009.

Jenkins, Philip. *The Next Christendom: The Coming of Global Christianity.* New York, NY: Oxford University Press, 2002.

Juell, Sheldon O. *Community Life in the Early Church.* Pasadena, CA: Koinonia Press, 1999.

Kinnaman, D., and G. Lyons. *UnChristian: What a New Generation Really Thinks about Christianity and Why It Matters.* Grand Rapids, MI: Baker Books, 2007.

Knechtel, Ronald C. and Dick L. Kranendonk. *2008 Charities Handbook: Income Tax, Fundraising, Accounting and Employment.* Elmira, ON: Canadian Council of Christian Charities, 2004.

Kranendonk, Dick L. *Serving as a Board Member: Protecting Yourself from Legal Liability While Serving Charities.* Belleville, ON: Essence Publishing, 2002.

Linthicum, Robert C. *City of God, City of Satan: A Biblical Theology of the Urban Church.* Grand Rapids, MI: Zondervan, 1991.

Linthicum, Robert C. *Transforming Power: Biblical Strategies for Making a Difference in Your Community.* Downers Grove, IL: InterVarsity Press, 2003.

McDowell, J., and D.H. Bellis. *The Last Christian Generation: The Crisis is Real. The Responsibility Ours.* Holiday, FL: Green Key Books, 2006.

McLaren, Brian D. *The Church on The Other Side.* Grand Rapids, MI: Zondervan, 1998.

Malloch, Theodore R. *Spiritual Enterprise: Doing Virtuous Business.* New York, NY: Encounter Books, 2008.

Marshall, Tom. *Understanding Leadership.* Kent, WA: Sovereign World, 1991.

Mattera, Joseph. *Ruling in the Gates: Preparing the Church to Transform Cities.* Lake Mary, FL: Creation House, 2003.

Maxwell, John. *Partners In Prayer.* Nashville, TN: Thomas Nelson Publishers, 1996.

Metro Vancouver, "Metro Vancouver, Population by Ethnic Origin, 2011, NHS"http://www.metrovancouver.org/about/publications/Publications/PopulationbyEthnicOriginNHS2011.pdf (accessed July 4, 2014)

Murray, Stuart. *City Vision: A Biblical View.* London, UK: Daybreak, 1990.

Neighbour Jr., Ralph W. "How to Create an Urban Strategy." In *Planting and Growing Urban Churches: From Dream to Reality.* Edited by Harvie M. Conn. Grand Rapids, MI: Baker Book House Company, 1997.

____. *Where Do We Go From Here? A Guidebook from The Cell Group Church.* Houston, TX: Touch, 1990.

Newbigin, Lesslie. *The Gospel in a Pluralist Society.* Grand Rapids, MI: William B. Eerdmans Publishing Company, 1989.

Niebuhr, H. Richard. *Christ & Culture*. San Francisco, CA: HarperSanFrancisco, 2001.

Page, Don. *Servant Empowered Leadership: A Hands-on Guide to Transforming You and Your Organization*. Langley, BC: Power to Change, 2009.

Pierce, Michael D. *120 Days of Prayer for our City Booklet*. London, UK: 1996.

Portnoy, Gary, and Judy Hart. "Where Everybody Knows Your Name – Cheers Lyrics." Lyrics on Demand. http://www.lyricsondemand.com/tvthemes/cheerslyrics.html (accessed March 30, 2010).

Primeau, Lee. *Mission Shift: Great Commission Living in a Postmodern World*. Mississauga, ON: The Master's Foundation, 2003.

Proudfoot, Shannon. "One in Five Canadian Residents Foreign Born; Percentage of Country's Immigrants Highest since Depression, Census Finds." *The Vancouver Sun,* December 5, 2007.

Pue, Carson. *Mentoring Leaders: Wisdom for Developing Character, Calling, and Competency*. Grand Rapids, MI: Baker Books, 2005.

Ravenhill, Leonard. *Revival Praying*. Bloomington, MN: Bethany House Publishers, 1981.

___. *Why Revival Tarries*. Minneapolis, MN: Bethany House Publishers, 1982.

Robinson, B.A. "Religion Data from the 2001 Canadian Census," Religious Tolerance, http://www.religioustolerance.org/can_rel0.htm (accessed March 30, 2010).

Schaeffer, Francis A. *Death in the City*. Downers Grove, IL: InterVarsity Press, 1969.

Smith, Oswald J. *The Passion for Souls*. Burlington, ON: Welch Publishing, 1986.

Straight.com – News. "Total number of homeless in Vancouver remains steady at 1,600," http://www.straight.com/news/499576/total-number-homeless-vancouver-remains-steady-1600 (accessed July 31, 2014).

Sumrall, Lester. *Secrets of Answered Prayer*. South Bend, IN: Sumrall Publishing, 1987.

Todd, Douglas, and Nicholas Read. "Our Religious Beliefs: Less Formal, More Diverse: Catholicism Still Leads, but the Number of Non-Christian is Growing Sharply." *The Vancouver Sun*, May 14, 2003.

Torrey, R.A. *The Power of Prayer*. Grand Rapids, MI: Zondervan, 1924.

Towns, Elmer L. *Fasting for Spiritual Breakthroughs*. Ventura, CA: Regal Books, 1996.

Turner, Steve. *A Vision for Christians in the Arts*. Downers Grove, IL: InterVarsity Press, 2001.

Twenge, Jean M. *Generation Me. Why Today's Young Americans Are More Confident, Assertive, Entitled–and More Miserable Than Ever Before*. New York, NY: Free Press, 2006.

Van Engen, Charles. *God's Missionary People: Rethinking The Purpose of the Local Church*. Grand Rapids, MI: Baker Books, 1991.

Van Gelder, Craig. *The Essence of the Church: A Community Created by the Spirit*. Grand Rapids, MI: Baker Books, 2000.

Vancouver.com. "Vancouver Districts and Neighbourhood Profiles and Maps." http://www.vancouver.com/real_estate/reloca-tion_tips/neighbourhoods_and_maps/#west- e n d (accessed March 30, 2010).

Vancouver Condo Info. "GVRD House Prices and Local Income." Vancouver Condo Info. http://vancouvercondo.info/2009/09/gvrd-house-prices-and-local-incomes.html (Accessed March 30, 2010).

VidOpp Video Contest Clearinghouse. "Online Video Stats Continue to Climb." The Video Contest Community. http://vidopp.com/2010/01/31/online-video-stats-continue-to-climb/ (Accessed March 30, 2010).

Wagner, Peter C. *Acts of the Holy Spirit.* Ventura, CA: Regal Books, 2000.

____. *Warfare Prayer: How to Seek God's Protection in the Battle to Build His Kingdom.* Ventura, CA: Regal Books, 1992.

____. *The Church in the Workplace: How God's People Can Transform Society.* Ventura, CA: Regal Books, 2006.

Willard, Dallas. *The Spirit of The Disciplines: Understanding How God Changes Lives.* New York, NY: Harper San Francisco, 1988.

Notes

Chapter 1

1   Government of Canada, "NHS Focus on Geography Series- Greater Vancouver, 2011," Statistics Canada, http://www12.statcan.gc.ca/nhs-enm/2011/as-sa/fogs-spg/Pages/FOG.cfm?lang=E&level=4&GeoCode=5915020 (accessed June 25, 2014).

2   David E. Bloom and Tarun Khanna, "The Urban Revolution," *Finance and Development, A Quarterly Magazine of the IMF,* September 2007, <u>http://www.imf.org/external/pubs/ft/fandd/2007/09/bloom.htm</u> (accessed March 30, 2010).

Chapter 2

3   Douglas Todd and Nicholas Read, "Our Religious Beliefs: Less Formal, More Diverse: Catholicism Still Leads, but the Number of Non-Christian is Growing Sharply," *The Vancouver Sun*, May 14, 2003.

4   Ronald C. Knechtel, and Dick L. Kranendonk, *2008 Charities Handbook: Income Tax, Fundraising, Accounting and Employment* (Elmira, ON:Canadian Council of Christian Charities, 2004).

5   Dick L. Kranendonk, *Serving as a Board Member: Protecting Yourself from Legal Liability While Serving Charities* (Belleville, ON: Essence Publishing, 2002).

6   Maggie Chandler, "West End Real State Analysis," Vancouver Reflections, www.vancouverreflections.com/category/west-end/ (accessed March 30, 2010).

7   BizMapBC, The Vancouver Economic Development Commission, "Downtown Vancouver (DVBIA) Neighbourhood Profile, 2009," under "Figure 9: Household Income Summary," http://www.bizmapbc.com/neighbourhood-profiles/down-town-neighbourhood.pdf (accessed March 30, 2010), 4.

8   B.A Robinson, "Religion Data from the 2001 Canadian Census," Religious Tolerance, http://www.religioustolerance.org/can_rel0.htm (accessed March 30, 2010)

9   Vancouver.com, "Vancouver Districts and Neighbourhood Profiles and Maps," http://www.vancouver.com/real_estate/relo-cation_tips/neighbourhoods_and_maps/#west-end (accessed March 30, 2010)

10   BizMapBC, The Vancouver Economic Development Comission, "Downtown Vancouver (DVBIA) Neighbourhood Profile, 2009," under "Figure 7: Education Levels," http://www.bizmapbc.com/neighbourhood-profiles/downtown-neighbour-hood.pdf (accessed March 30, 2010), 4.

11   BizMapBC, The Vancouver Economic Development Commission, "Downtown Vancouver (DVBIA) Neighbourhood Profile, 2009," under "Figure 7: Education Levels," http://www.bizmapbc.com/neighbourhood-profiles/downtown-neighbour-hood.pdf (accessed March 30, 2010), 4.

12   Metro Vancouver, "Metro Vancouver, Population by Ethnic Origin, 2011, NHS" http://www.metrovancouver.org/about/publications/Publications/PopulationbyEthnicOriginNHS2011.pdf (accessed July 4, 2014)

13   BizMapBC, "Downtown Vancouver (DVBIA) Neighbourhood Profile, 2009," The Vancouver Economic Development Commission, under "Family Structure," http://www.bizmapbc.com/neighbourhood-profiles/downtown-neigh-bourhood.pdf (accessed March 30, 2010).

* "Family is defined as a census family – a married couple, com-mon-law couple, or lone-parent with a child or youth who is under the age of 25 and who does not have his or her own spouse or child in the household. Married couples and common-law couples may or may not have such children and youth living with them"

14   First Baptist Church, BC, "Ministry Plan. Final Report of the 20/20 Vision Renewal Committee for 2006/07" (Report presented to the Church Council of First Baptist Church, Vancouver, BC, February 2007), 7. // Source: Data from BizMapBC, "Downtown Vancouver (DVBIA) Neighbourhood Profile, 2009," The Vancouver Economic Development Commission, under "Population," http://www.bizmapbc.com/neighbourhood-profiles/downtown-neighbourhood.pdf (accessed July 7, 2014).

15   Maggie Chandler, "Vancouver Real State Analysis," Vancouver Reflections, http://www.vancouverreflections.com/ (Accessed March 30, 2010)

16   Vancouver.com, "Vancouver Districts and Neighbourhood Profiles and Maps," http://www.vancouver.com/real_estate/relocation_tips/neighbourhoods_and_maps/#west-end (accessed March 30, 2010)

17   Vancouver.com, "Vancouver Districts and Neighbourhood Profiles and Maps," http://www.vancouver.com/real_estate/relocation_tips/neighbourhoods_and_maps/#west-end (accessed March 30, 2010).

18   First Baptist Church, BC, "Ministry Plan. Final Report of the 20/20 Vision Renewal Committee for 2006/07," (Report presented to the Church Council of First Baptist Church, Vancouver, BC, February 2007), 7.

19   Vancouver.com, "Vancouver Districts and Neighbourhood Profiles and Maps," http://www.vancouver.com/real_estate/relocation_tips/neighbourhoods_and_maps/#west-end (accessed March 30, 2010).

20   Metro Vancouver, "Metro Vancouver, Population by Ethnic Origin, 2011, NHS" http://www.metrovancouver.org/about/

publications/Publications/PopulationbyEthnicOriginNHS2011. pdf (accessed July 4, 2014)

21 BizMapBC, The Vancouver Economic Development Commission, "Downtown Vancouver (DVBIA) Neighbourhood Profile, 2009", under "Overview," http://www.bizmapbc.com/ neighbourhood-profiles/downtown-neighbourhood.pdf (accessed March 30, 2010), 1.

22 Campus Crusade for Christ, "The Jesus Film – Video," http://www.campuscrusade.com/Jesus_Film/2_hour_jesus_ video.htm (accessed March 30, 2010).

23 Gary Portnoy and Judy Hart, "Where Everybody Knows Your Name – Cheers Lyrics," Lyrics on Demand, http://www.lyr-icsondemand.com/tvthemes/cheerslyrics.html (accessed March 30, 2010).

24 BizMapBC, The Vancouver Economic Development Commission, "Downtown Vancouver (DVBIA) Neighbourhood Profile, 2009", under "Figure 9: Household Income Summary,"http://www.bizmapbc.com/neighbourhood-profiles/ downtown-neighbourhood.pdf (accessed July, 2014), 4.

25 First Baptist Church, BC, "Ministry Plan. Final Report of the 20/20 Vision Renewal Committee for 2006/07" (Report presented to the Church Council of First Baptist Church, Vancouver, BC, February 2007), 5.

26 BizMapBC, The Vancouver Economic Development Commission, "Downtown Vancouver (DVBIA) Neighbourhood Profile, 2009", under "Level of Education," http://www.bizmapbc. com/neighbourhood-profiles/downtown-neighbourhood.pdf (accessed March 30, 2010), 4.

27 Steve Turner, *A Vision for Christians in the Arts* (Downers Grove, IL: InterVarsity Press, 2001), 20.

28 Ralph W. Neighbour Jr., "How to Create an Urban Strategy," *Where Do We Go From Here?* (Houston, TX: Touch, 1990) quoted in Harvie M. Conn, ed., *Planting and Growing Urban Churches: From Dream to Reality* (Grand Rapids, MI: Baker Book House Company, 1997), 112.

Chapter 3

29   Robert C. Linthicum, *City of God, City of Satan: A Biblical Theology of the Urban Church* (Grand Rapids, MI: Zondervan, 1991), 148.

30   Straight.com – News, "Total number of homeless in Vancouver remains steady at 1,600," http://www.straight.com/news/499576/total-number-homeless-vancouver-remains-steady-1600 (accessed July 31, 2014).

31   Ibid.

Chapter 4

32   Ralph W. Neighbour Jr., *Where Do We Go From Here? A Guidebook From The Cell Group Church* (Houston, TX: Touch, 1990), 137.

33   R.A. Torrey, *The Power of Prayer* (Grand Rapids, MI: Zondervan, 1924), 16.

34   Ralph Herring, *Circle of Prayer* (Wheaton, IL: Tyndale House Publishers, 1974), 8.

35   Leonard Ravenhill, *Revival Praying* (Bloomington, MN: Bethany House Publishers, 1981), 124.

36   Leonard Ravenhill, *Why Revival Tarries* (Minneapolis, MN: Bethany House Publishers, 1982), 18.

37   Peter Wagner, *Warfare Prayer: How to Seek God's Protection in the Battle to Build His Kingdom* (Ventura, CA: Regal Books, 1992), 65.

38   John Maxwell, *Partners In Prayer* (Nashville, TN: Thomas Nelson Publishers, 1996), 79.

39   Jim Cymbala, *Fresh Power: What Happens When God Leads and You Follow* (Grand Rapids, MI: Zondervan, 2001), 142.

40   Lester Sumrall, *Secrets of Answered Prayer* (South Bend, IN: Sumrall Publishing, 1987), 88.

41   6S Marketing, "Infographic: Canadian Internet Usage Statistics on Mobile, Search and Social" http://www.6smarketing.com/blog/infographic-canadian-internet-usage-statistics/ (Accessed July 7, 2014)

42 Cindy Jacobs, *Possessing the Gates of the Enemy* (Grand Rapids, MI: Baker Publishing Group, 2009), 157.

43 John Maxwell, 7.

44 Dick Eastman, *Change the World School of Prayer* (Studio City, CA: World Literature Crusade, 1976), D33.

45 Peter Wagner, *Acts of the Holy Spirit* (Ventura, CA: Regal Books, 2000), 126.

46 Block, Peter, *Stewardship: Choosing Service Over Self-Interest* (Berret-Koehler Publishers, 1993), 42.